THE UNVARNISHED TRUTH

THE UNVARNISHED TRUTH

Purpose in the Pain

Dr. Karla Hylton

First published in Jamaica, 2023
by Karla Hylton

© 2023 Karla Hylton

ISBN 978-976-97176-0-2 (hbk)
ISBN 978-976-97176-1-9 (pbk)
ISBN 978-976-97176-2-6 (e-book)

**Cataloguing-In-Publication Data available
at the National Library of Jamaica**

Cover and Book Design by Christina Moore Fuller
Front Cover Illustration by Md Imtiaz Jony

Printed and Bound in the United States of America

Dedication

To my beloved family and friends, this narrative is dedicated with heartfelt appreciation for your support and love. You have been my guiding lights, illuminating my path through life's challenges. May this, my story, serve as a tribute to the indomitable human spirit which fuels our resilience and fortitude in the face of adversity.

Contents

Disclaimer

This autobiographical work was inspired by actual events and persons. However, some of the characters and incidents portrayed and the names used are fictitious, and any similarity of those fictitious characters or incidents to the name, character or history of any actual person, living or dead, or any actual event is entirely coincidental or unintentional.

This narrative reflects my personal perspective and interpretations of the events and people in my life. Others involved may have different viewpoints or memories that vary from my own.

The information and advice provided in this book are intended for general informational purposes only and should not be considered a substitute for professional mental health or medical advice, diagnosis or treatment. The author is not a licensed mental health professional, therapist, or medical doctor, and the content of this book does not constitute a therapeutic relationship.

Acknowledgments

First and foremost, my heartfelt gratitude goes to the Almighty God for His steadfast guidance and constant presence throughout this journey.

To my beloved family and cherished friends, whose presence has accompanied me through every triumph and tribulation, I express my deepest gratitude. You are my true tribe.

To my beloved children, you are, and forever will be, my greatest accomplishment, and my love for you knows no bounds.

With love, this acknowledgment is dedicated to each and every one of you.

Prologue

Our past experiences woven with both moments of joy and pain, hold within them invaluable lessons that act as guiding lights in shaping our future choices. Each encounter, whether uplifting or challenging, serves as a teacher, enlightening us on the significance of discernment, self-preservation and the true nature of compassion.

We learn that true compassion extends far beyond the realm of material support. It is a balance of empathy and self-care, respecting personal boundaries and trusting our God-given intuition. These lessons form a foundation to uplift others and make a lasting, positive impact on the world.

Inevitably, we encounter moments of despair, where the weight of life's challenges becomes almost unbearable. For some, as was the case with me, this darkness may lead to the depths of suicidal ideation, where hope feels distant and elusive. Yet, it is within these very moments that the power of resilience and the human spirit shine brightest.

As I reflect upon my story, I observe firsthand the destructive impact of narcissism on the foundation of trust. It is a corrosive force that erodes the underpinnings of love and compassion, substituting them with a hollow shell of superficiality. The narcissist's web of deceit woven with precision, ensnares their victims in a mesh of confusion, self-doubt and emotional turmoil.

The loss of trust does not signify our weakness or gullibility. Rather, it serves as a testament to our capacity to believe in the goodness of others, and to extend our hearts in vulnerability. It is a reminder that not everyone we encounter will honor that trust.

Suicidal ideation is a subject most often avoided. It is a subject I will speak about. Overcoming these thoughts demands an unyielding resilience—a tenacity that stands against the lure of death. It is a testament to the indomitable nature of the human will, a declaration that even in the darkest of times, there is a flicker of light that can guide us towards a path of healing and transformation.

Those who have battled through the depths of such hopelessness understand the convoluted layers of pain, isolation, and the struggle to find purpose. Rising out of this abyss requires immense courage and vulnerability to reach out for support, seek professional help, and engage in the healing process. During this arduous climb, individuals learn about self-reliance, self-compassion and forgiveness. It involves rediscovering identity and purpose, and nurturing a renewed appreciation for life's preciousness.

As survivors of suicidal thoughts, we hold a strength forged in deep despair, becoming examples of hope for fellow travelers. Our compassion, understanding and support guide those lost in their own pain's maze.

Through sharing my personal story openly, my aim is to foster safe spaces for meaningful conversations, eradicating the stigma surrounding mental health and instilling hope in those who may feel trapped in their own desolation.

My narrative transcends time as I delve into the trauma stemming from familial dysfunction and the anguish experienced in a marriage with a narcissistic individual. Furthermore, I navigate the uncharted territory of estrangement from my own children and the ensuing heartache it brings.

These pages recount a journey that has traversed the heights of joy and plumbed the depths of despair. Every twist and turn, every triumph and setback, has sculpted the contours of who I am today. Through the moments of heartbreak and disillusionment to the instances where fragments of light pierce through the darkness, my spirit evolved.

Along this journey, the hand of God has always been a guiding force, directing my course even in the face of unimaginable suffering. It stands as proof to the undeniable truth that within the depths of adversity, a divine light persists, leading us toward the end of the tunnel.

May this story serve as an illumination for those who have faced their own trials, a testament to the power of embracing our experiences as catalysts for growth. Through these words, I invite you to join me on a pilgrimage of self-discovery, as together we explore the intricate dance between pain and purpose, ultimately discovering that even in the darkest moments, the light of purpose can guide us home.

This is my story.

Introduction

*M*onsters! They may seem like a figment of imagination, yet they are ever-present in the shadows of our lives. They manifest in different forms and shapes. You can sleep with them, share meals with them, play with them, make love to them, share a life with them, have children, build a house or even establish a business.

Their presence may go unnoticed for years as they wear a mask of charm and deceit, obscuring their true nature. Unfortunately, when the veil is lifted, it can be too late and our lives can be irreparably damaged.

No one enters into marriage anticipating or planning for divorce. We enter into our marriages with hope and dreams of eternal happiness believing we are exempt from the harsh realities faced by others. We envision our lives as fairy tales where happily ever after is the inevitable ending. But life has a way of shattering those illusions, exposing the monsters that can reside within even the most enchanting relationships.

Monsters are not merely creatures of myth or legend. They are an unfortunate reality that can infiltrate our lives. By the time we realize their true nature, we may find ourselves trapped in their clutches, too beaten down to escape the darkness that surrounds them. Such was the case with my ex-husband.

I had the typical fairy tale marriage... or so it appeared to the outside world. The picture-perfect couple, the envy of many, with smiles plastered on our faces and a seemingly idyllic life. I wore the mask of a contented wife, deceiving not only others but also myself. I convinced myself that everything was fine, that the cracks beneath the surface were mere illusions, easily dismissed. How else could I have coped with the harsh reality that awaited me?

Deep down, I knew there were unsettling moments, subtle signs that whispered of discontent. I pushed those doubts aside, a delicate dance of denial and self-preservation. I clung to the remnants of the fairy tale I so desperately wanted to believe in. I buried my doubts under layers of false optimism, hoping that if I pretended hard enough, reality would bend to my will.

In retrospect, I realize that my ability to deceive myself was born out of a combination of fear, societal pressures and the desire to maintain the illusion of a perfect marriage. I was afraid of facing the truth head-on, afraid of the consequences it might bring. Admitting that all was not well meant acknowledging the unravelling of the fairy tale, the dismantling of the carefully constructed façade.

The narcissist wears a mask and is the perfect actor, the perfect liar, the perfect pretender, because... that's all it was... the perfect lie. Narcissists possess the innate ability to fool everyone and is a testament to their prowess in the art of deception. The repercussions of narcissism reverberate through the fabric of one's self-worth, creating a fertile ground for self-doubt and insecurity to take root.

As time progresses, the mask inevitably slips, revealing their true nature. When the marriage comes to its end, their vindictiveness becomes starkly apparent, leaving no doubt about the brutality of their actions for all to witness.

I am no idiot. My brain works perfectly well. I have even achieved academically. I have common sense. I have no known disabilities. Despite this, I was no match for the venom and the evil spewed by the monster.

My ex-husband is not the first monster I have met. I have met many, but he was definitely the one I spent the most time with. He possessed the ability to break my spirit and strip away the very things I cherished the most.

It pains me to admit that I willingly gave him the power he wielded against me, as I handed over control and allowed him to manipulate and govern my life. This relinquishment of power had dire consequences, as it granted him the authority to diminish my sense of self-worth and stifle my voice.

The experiences I had during the marriage has taught me the importance of safeguarding my own power and not surrendering it to others, for I now understand that my worth should never be dependent on someone else's approval or control.

CHAPTER 1

Glimpses of the Monster

*W*ithin my community, I was perceived as belonging to a well-to-do family, and my academic performance earned me the label of an outstanding student. Despite these accolades my peers often dubbed me the 'ice princess' due to my reserved and introverted nature. My shyness, love for books and limited social circle led to a lack of close friendships.

Nurtured in a household rich with Eastern traditions, rules and values, my East Indian heritage dictated that I steer clear of any associations with boys or the mere notion of having a boyfriend until I reached the age of eighteen. Consequently, it was not until I reached this milestone that I embarked on a relationship with my future husband.

I had known him since we were both six years old but even though we attended the same school for years, it was not until much later that a friendship developed between us. In those earlier years, I considered him a 'bad boy' at the school, deterring any interest on my part. He did not strike me as the studious type and often appeared to be a rule-breaker. As I approached eighteen, I found myself becoming the focal point of his attention.

Our love story began at a key moment in my life in the year 1987. I had just begun my transition into tertiary education in the city of Kingston. Coincidentally, he too had relocated to Kingston after securing a job there. My husband-to-be made it his mission to visit me at the University where I resided in the campus lodgings.

During those early days of dating, the university became the backdrop to our blossoming romance, and the shared experience of pursuing our respective dreams in the same city added a unique charm to our relationship. His thoughtful gestures, such as visiting me often and gifting me with my favourite chocolates, left a lasting impression on my heart, and it was during those moments that the foundation of our story began to take shape.

He was a struggling young man and at the time did not have much money left over for fancy dates or outings. Instead, our dates were characterized by his visits and leisurely walks in the gardens near my residence. I looked forward to his visits and enjoyed spending time with him. He emanated warmth and tenderness, providing invaluable emotional support during this transformative period when I was distanced from the familiar comforts of home.

The year 1988 was momentous, as Hurricane Gilbert ravaged our nation, leaving a trail of unforgettable devastation. In the aftermath, circumstances forced us to endure a prolonged period of separation. While the University remained closed, I had to remain home in Morant Bay, while he stayed in Kingston, where work still demanded his presence.

The consequences of the hurricane brought additional challenges, as we were left without electricity and the telecommunication system was severely affected. Amid this isolating and trying time, my boyfriend displayed a touching gesture of love. Unable to communicate through the usual means, he took to writing love letters each day, preserving them as a collection to share with me in person when we reunited. These love letters became a source of comfort during our separation.

In general, our time together as a couple before marriage was filled with beautiful moments, shared experiences and the occasional squabbles. After two years of dating, we made the decision to take our relationship to the next level and get married. There was not a grand, elaborate proposal; rather, it came about naturally through meaningful discussions we had.

Influenced by the values and family structure I grew up with, I held a belief that it was essential to honor the sanctity of marriage. Moreover, the dream of marriage had always held a special place in my heart, and I desired a family founded on love, respect, and freedom from dysfunction.

The choice to marry went beyond a mere declaration of love; it was a deliberate step towards building a strong foundation for a future filled with fulfillment and harmony. Deep within me, there was an earnest yearning for children and a family that would be vastly different from the one I had grown up in. The vision of a loving and cohesive family became a driving force in my decision-making process. I saw it as a chance to break free from any patterns of dysfunction that might have lingered from both our pasts and to intentionally build a life filled with happiness, understanding, and mutual respect.

However, as my story unfolded it became apparent that this was not to be so. The first time I became acutely aware that something was wrong, was around the time we became engaged.   Looking back, I realize that my naivety and low self-esteem left me vulnerable, even desperate, which led me to pardon an incident that, in hindsight, should not have been overlooked.

My boyfriend told me that he had only one sibling, a younger brother whom I had already met.   His brother Frank, was a struggling student at his high school. In fact, my boyfriend asked me to assist with his education and I happily agreed to do so. Unknowingly, I was embarking on an early journey into the world of tutoring.

I began picking Frank up from a designated location and bringing him to my abode, where I took on the role of his tutor in language and mathematics. It was a characteristic of my nature to extend a helping hand, driven by a blend of goodness and innocence that sometimes made me vulnerable and codependent.

The untainted truth came to light during a significant occasion when my parents hosted a meeting with my boyfriend's parents at our home in Morant Bay, St. Thomas. As my mom engaged in conversation with his mother, the truth emerged, contradicting what I had been told.

Contrary to my boyfriend's claim of having only one sibling, it surfaced that he was, in fact, the second child among five siblings (same mother, same father), all residing in the same household.

I was in utter disbelief on hearing this bit of news. I struggled to comprehend why such an inconsequential detail would be concealed from me. What significance would it hold if he had four siblings instead of one? It felt like an unnecessary breach of trust.

While I can only speculate on the true motive behind this deception, my boyfriend's explanation failed to provide a logical or credible reason. I surmised that he held some deep sense of shame or embarrassment concerning the existence of these three siblings he had kept concealed from me. I could not help but wonder if his insecurities about his own self-worth had driven him to fabricate this lie.

A red flag was raised, signaling a warning that all was not as it seemed. While my mother rightfully expressed alarm and caution, I foolishly dismissed her concerns. I allowed myself to be swayed by the desire to keep this man in my life, finding ease in his presence in spite of the significant crack that had formed in our trust.

Looking back, I realize the gravity of my innocence and the extent to which I had become enmeshed in a web of deceit, compromising my own well-being in the process. I was already showing signs of codependence.

Without trust, the very essence of a meaningful relationship is compromised. I now realize that had I possessed the wisdom to see beyond my emotions, the right course of action would have been to end the relationship at that very moment, preventing it from progressing to the stage of marriage.

It wasn't that his lie in itself was exceptionally damaging or significant, but rather, it was the ease with which he lied and the utterly unnecessary nature of the deception that shook the core of my trust in him.

While I firmly believe in the power of forgiveness, I recognize the importance of entering the sacred bond of marriage with a clear conscience. Perhaps engaging in couples counseling could have been beneficial, helping us address any lingering misunderstandings and confront the hurt I experienced, while also exploring the reasons behind his deception. Open communication and understanding could have been the keys to healing and strengthening our bond as we embarked on this new chapter together.

Now, with hindsight as my guide, I realize that this deception was the first glimpse of a dark presence creeping into our relationship – manipulation and control – revealing themselves in our interactions. Had I recognized and acknowledged these signs, it could have spared me from the detrimental consequences that lay ahead on the road we eventually walked together.

But life is an adventure of learning, and I have now come to recognize the value of trust as a non-negotiable pillar in any relationship. It is the very essence that binds hearts and souls together, and without it, the strength of a connection is severely compromised.

As my intuition screamed at me to let go, I foolishly chose to silence its voice. The consequences of ignoring our intuition are significant. Our intuition and gut feelings act as a guiding compass, offering insights that may elude our rational mind. We must learn to heed these whispers.

There were a few arguments as I sought explanation for the lies that had been told, with no real resolution. I eventually blocked out the incident. I repressed the memory.

In spite of this, the human brain has a way of preserving experiences and memories that cannot be easily erased. They may linger in the depths concealed but always present, waiting to resurface.

On the financial front, my husband-to-be came from a disadvantaged background. His struggles as a young child and teenager touched my heart and I felt overwhelming compassion for him. He, like me, had a dysfunctional family structure. His parents' relationship was stormy and led to periods of separation, with children outside the marriage further complicating the dynamics.

I listened to him recount traumatic experiences of being left alone at home for extended periods, with no knowledge of his parents' whereabouts. These heart-wrenching accounts opened my eyes to the resilience he displayed in the face of adversity and undoubtedly played a role in deepening my love and compassion for him.

Driven by empathy and perhaps a touch of gullibility, I willingly extended a helping hand long before our marriage. There were instances when my husband-to-be found himself without a place to call home, and I, without hesitation, offered him refuge in those challenging times.

My inclination to assist was born out of love and a genuine desire to alleviate his struggles and offer him solace during times of turmoil. I've never been one to be captivated by money or people who exude wealth. Rather, I find inspiration in ambition and personal growth. While I certainly appreciate and desire the finer things in life, I believe that they should never overshadow the pursuit of meaningful goals and good character.

Naturally, my parents had valid concerns about his financial capability, but my perspective differed. I saw his ambition and was determined to stand by his side, supporting his aspirations.

Encouragingly, I urged him to pursue the subjects required for his dream of becoming a chartered accountant, even during times of deterrence, when he did not want to do so. My belief in his potential led me to cheer him on, desiring nothing but the best for him. My deepest wish was to witness his great success. Little did I anticipate that success would bring out the monster in him.

My parents also harbored reservations about the ethnicity of my future husband, as he is of African descent. Due to cultural influences, they were hesitant about accepting a mixed marriage, as their own marriage had been arranged in a more traditional setting. Back in their time, mixed-race couples faced disapproval from certain quarters. Despite these reservations, my parents chose to prioritize my happiness and ultimately embraced my fiancé as my chosen partner.

I recognize that it was not easy for my parents to overcome their cultural beliefs and preconceptions. They had grown up in a society where traditions were deeply ingrained, and the idea of marrying someone from a different background was met with skepticism. The concept of love marriages, especially across ethnic lines, was something they had never experienced firsthand.

My husband and I got married on New Year's Day, 1992. It was a beautiful wedding financed by my family as was customary in those days. There were approximately two hundred guests most of whom were my parents' invitees.

We had one car which was gifted to me years before by my parents. My parents continued to finance me to an extent during the early months and years of my marriage. I was still a student in university, studying for my doctorate degree in Biotechnology which I completed in 1995.

I don't remember much during the first year of my marriage. I do know that my husband worked and studied for most of that time. As I reflect upon those days now, a lingering doubt surfaces, leaving me uncertain as to whether it was truly work that kept him away from home or if there were other forces at play concealed beneath the surface.

At that time, I accepted the explanations I was given, unaware of the web of deception that was beginning to weave its way into our relationship. Little did I know that seeds of narcissism had been sown, taking root in the soil of mistrust and casting a shadow over our future together.

As I venture into the exploration of unraveling the complex kaleidoscope of my life story, I am confronted with the resounding truth that trust is the bedrock upon which all healthy relationships are built. It serves as the vital glue that binds two individuals, enabling them to construct a life rooted in authenticity, transparency and mutual devotion.

Trust is the bedrock of healthy relationships.

CHAPTER 2

The Early Years

*S*o, now I find myself replaying the record of my life, delving into the depths of my childhood, searching for the roots that may have inadvertently led me into the clutches of a narcissist. It is often said that victims of narcissistic abuse share common traits and are often products of dysfunctional families.

In the year 1969, I entered this world. My early years were shaped on a sugar plantation, its roots tracing back to the era of slavery. With pride, I identify as a true native of Jamaica.

As I reflect on my formative years, I cannot ignore the shadows that lingered over my upbringing. I had a childhood laced with moments of both joy and adversity. I was the first of four children and the only daughter of my parents. I grew up with my father's alcoholism and was witness to many acts of domestic violence. My dad was also openly unfaithful to my mom.

Perhaps, my childhood prepared me to be a compliant wife. It was the breeding ground for my codependency, a trait commonly found in those who grow up in the shadows of addiction. Regardless of my father's struggle with alcoholism, my affection for him remained unswerving.

The early experiences of family dysfunction sculpted the landscape of my psyche, influencing my perception of love, trust and my own self-worth. The patterns of disharmonious relationships became my normal, ingrained in the very fabric of my being. I did not know at the time that these patterns would continue to ripple through my life attracting me to the familiar territory of dysfunctional relationships. It is clear that my childhood served as a crucial foundation, laying the groundwork for the toxic dynamics I would later encounter.

The wounds that formed within me, both seen and unseen, created my vulnerability, opening the door for the manipulation and control that a narcissist so skillfully exploits.

There's not much to tell as I traverse my early years. The mind has the amazing capacity to block out memories as it chooses, selective amnesia as it is called. I don't know if there are events in my mind that need to be forgotten. I just know that I can have an excellent memory in certain situations and then zilch in others. This unique ability is still with me. I do not consciously select what to remember and what to forget; my brain makes the decision.

My therapist later explained that selective amnesia is a curious phenomenon of the human mind, where certain memories or experiences are intentionally forgotten or suppressed. It is as if a veil is drawn over specific events, shielding them from conscious recollection. This intriguing defense mechanism often arises as a response to traumatic or distressing situations, allowing individuals to protect themselves from emotional pain.

While selective amnesia can provide temporary relief, it also hinders personal growth and healing. Understanding the complexities of this fascinating psychological process sheds light on the multifarious workings of our minds and reminds us of the delicate balance between remembering and forgetting as a mode of self-preservation.

With this understanding, I step into a deeper exploration of my experiences, beginning with an event that transpired during my infancy – an encounter with trauma that, because of my age at the time, eludes conscious memory.

I was merely six months old when I became

gravely ill and was admitted in the hospital in the parish that I was living in. I am told that I was on the verge of death, when my Godmother, a nurse, instructed my parents to remove me from that hospital and take me to the only Children's hospital in Jamaica, The Bustamante Hospital for Children, located miles away from where I was. My parents took on the two-hour trip with an ailing child feeding me ice chips on the way.

On arrival to the hospital, the nurses on duty, seeing how sickly I was, allowed my parents to forgo the waiting and rushed me to a doctor on duty. I was diagnosed with severe gastroenteritis and was hospitalized for nine days.

Still, as I persistently affirm, divine providence weaves through this narrative. Years, even decades later, an unexpected turn of events would come to pass and I would find myself appointed as the Chairman of the Friends of the Bustamante Hospital for Children – the very institution that had years prior, orchestrated my rescue from the clutches of near-death.

Throughout my childhood and even early adulthood, I continued to be very susceptible to contracting gastroenteritis, as well as other infectious diseases. I was always at the doctor suffering from various ailments ranging from allergies, tonsillitis to suspected rheumatic fever. I was a very skinny child which I recall caused my parents much concern.

My parents moved to the parish of St. Thomas for careers on a sugar plantation when I was around two years old. Living on a sugar plantation was not all bad. The memories of dwelling in a plantation style house, nestled amidst sprawling open spaces, evoke a sense of freedom and curiosity that still resonates within me.

The allure of the outdoors has remained an enduring love affair throughout the chapters of my life. It is within the embrace of lush green grass and colorful gardens that I find my peace and inspiration. I feel a connection to nature that renews and rejuvenates my soul. Even now, I am drawn to the tranquility of gardens, to the vibrant colors and fragrant blooms that paint a masterpiece of beauty.

The outdoors was my safe space, and I loved to explore the vast grounds. We lived in three different locations on the plantation over the course of ten years. Notably, my dear brother John was born shortly after we moved to St. Thomas, when I was three years old.

At the tender age of five, I found myself thrust into the harrowing depths of a home invasion by nine armed men, an experience that still reverberates within me to this day. This haunting incident, while seemingly ripped from the pages of a Hollywood script, unfolded within the borders of my beloved Jamaica, a stark reminder of the complexities and fragilities of the world we inhabit. This traumatic experience left an indelible mark on my young spirit, forever shaping my perception of the world.

I will attempt to chronicle the events that took place that fateful night in August of 1974.

I was asleep in my bed which was located directly under vintage glass paned windows. The tranquility of the night interrupted as I was abruptly awakened by my father's urgent grip, lifting me from my slumber just as shards of glass rained down upon my pillow. In that fleeting moment, my father's swift actions had spared me from harm's reach.

With grim determination, my father whisked me away, carrying me swiftly to his bedroom. There, within the chaos that enveloped our home, he instructed my mother, my two-year-old brother John, and myself to seek refuge beneath their bed. It was a desperate attempt to shield us from the menacing presence that lurked outside our home.

In the hazy realm between sleep and wakefulness, I remained unaware of the unfolding events. As I became more alert, I realized that we were in the midst of a perilous situation. Nine armed men had converged upon our home, their sinister intentions veiled by the darkness of the night.

This explained the urgency with which my father had whisked me away from my sleep, his swift actions driven by an instinct to shield me from the impending danger. During those days, the concept of burglar grills had not become a standard feature in Jamaican homes and so it was not a difficult task for these criminals to gain entry. I would discover later that these same men had also mercilessly killed my beloved pet dog, Rusty.

To provide context for the events that occurred thereafter, it is essential to shed light on my parent's occupation on the sugar plantation. My father worked on the sugar plantation as a Crop Control Officer. To date, I am not really sure what that means but I do know he spent a lot of time driving from one sugar cane field to the next inspecting the sugarcane crop. He was also involved with managing the spraying of the cane fields with pesticides as well as fertilizer application.

My mom worked as the Cashier for the sugar company, which meant that she was entrusted with the keys to this enormous walk-in vault which safe guarded both stationary supplies as well as money. Every August, the company disbursed cash bonuses, resulting in a substantial amount of money being stored in this vault.

Unbeknownst to us, this gang of nine had meticulously orchestrated a plan to rob the sugar estate, fully aware of the cash earmarked for bonuses. Their scheme was methodical and well-organized, with the mastermind, the gang leader, hailing from a different country, adding an extra layer of complexity. Their intention was to have my mother open the large vault for them to gain entry to steal the cash.

So, to continue the saga, these men gained entry into my home. We were found under the bed and were told to come out. I recall one of the robbers searching through my mom's jewelry box and the gang leader saying, "We did not come to take anything from these people, leave it". He had some goodness in him.

We were taken to my father's pickup truck. They blind-folded my mom, put her in the passenger seat and handed her John to hold in her lap. They then tied up my dad and placed him to lie tummy down in the back of the truck. I was told to lay on top of my dad. We were driven uphill to unknown parts without streets and without street lights. We drove on dirt paths.

When they stopped, they removed my mom from the vehicle and handed baby John to me. John cried and cried and for some unknown reason, perhaps by the grace of God, the robbers handed baby John back to my mom and told her to stay. They disappeared into the darkness.

My mom was not tied up, she had only been blindfolded. She removed her blindfold and untied my dad. He went into the driver's seat and started the car engine. Immersed in utter darkness, our surroundings remained a mystery. The unsettling sound of gunshots reverberated through the air, indicating that we were in an undeveloped vicinity near the main office where the cash was stored.

Dad was still trying to get the car engine started when out of the darkness we saw headlights from three cars coming out of the blackness. Apparently, the criminals had already positioned their escape vehicles.

One gang member came out of the car with a knife in his hand. To this day I remember my dad saying in local dialect, "we dead now". He thought we were most certainly going to be killed. But not for the first time and most definitely not the last, God intervened.

The robber slashed the two back tires of our vehicle and went back into his own vehicle. He only wanted to slow us down. We drove with the flat tires, round and round until we saw a glimmer of light. My Dad drove towards the light until we could identify where we were.

The saga lasted about three hours and as you can imagine, to a little girl, this seemed forever. While, it ended with the robbers allowing us to go free, I still do not understand why they did not actually acquire the cash they were trying to steal.

In light of the gunshots that had been fired, the police were aware of the attempted robbery, prompting them to set up roadblocks in order to capture the criminals. Strangely, the police were unaware of my family's capture during the time of the ordeal. It was not until we reached civilized areas that the authorities were made aware of our plight.

The road blocks that were set up proved to be instrumental in the capture of the gang leader and other members of the gang, though not all the members were captured. We were later told that this was the first time, those high-powered weapons carried by the robbers were detected in the country.

As I retell this story, I can still feel the weight of my pounding heart, the trembling of my small frame as I bore witness to the intrusion of these nine armed men into the sanctuary of my home. In an instant, the familiar walls that once provided solace transformed into an arena of chaos, shattering the innocence of my childhood and imprinting upon my young spirit a sense of vulnerability, powerlessness and fragility.

While the ordeal eventually came to an end, its impact continued to reverberate through the years that followed. The echoes of that traumatic event became etched into my psyche, influencing my perceptions of safety and instilling within me a heightened sense of awareness.

The capture of the thieves started another series of traumatic episodes as my parents would have to leave myself and my brother with friends while they travelled the two-and-a-half-hour drive to the court. This occurred many times until the conviction of the perpetrators and caused renewed fear and anxiety each time my parents would have to leave. I feared that they would not return.

This tale, as incredulous as it may seem, is a reminder that the boundaries of reality are often stretched beyond our imagination. I am reminded that truth can indeed be stranger than fiction.

I am acutely aware that a higher power exists, irrespective of our individual interpretations and acknowledgments – whether we refer to this power as God or a Divine force. The guidance and shelter granted to us remains steadfast, even in the face of adversity. Through the toughest of moments, the presence of God is unwavering.

Experiencing such a traumatic event should never be underestimated, as it can deeply impact a child's development and shape their growing mind. The adults in this scenario also carried their own burdens of trauma. This incident occurred at a time when little was known about Post Traumatic Stress Disorder (PTSD) and the effects of trauma in my part of the world. Mental health remained a taboo subject and the availability of psychiatrists and psychologists were limited.

After the robbery, I actually never spent another night in that house. We were moved to another sugar plantation home on a hill called Peacock Hill. The hill top view was that of vast cane fields, the sugar factory and beyond I could see the blue turquoise waters of the Caribbean Sea. It was a nice house with lots and lots of outdoor space which I absolutely delighted in. My neighbors had children my age and so I would be allowed to walk from one house to another visiting playmates.

As a consequence of that harrowing experience, my mother was granted night security, which entailed having an armed guard present in our house for twelve hours each day. This constant and unnerving presence served as a chilling reminder that life was unsafe.

Life was unsafe.

CHAPTER 3

Lost Girl

*M*y new abode proved to be a sanctuary, offering an abundance of uncharted territories to discover and escapades to embrace. I found peace in the simple pleasure of pacing up and down the long pathway leading to my house while bouncing my ball, immersing myself in the tranquility of this solitary pastime.

In this serene backdrop, my father tended to a herd of goats and cultivated his own vegetable garden, where I gladly lent a hand in watering the gardens. To add to our self-sufficiency, we even had a stock pond where we grew fish for consumption.

Growing up, my parents held markedly distinct and strict views on my future. Their divergent visions often created a challenging and complex dynamic within our family.

My dad's expectations were very clear: do exceptionally well in school so that you attain financial independence, while my mom's expectations were: learn how to clean and cook exceptionally well so that you please your future husband. Caught between these conflicting perspectives, I found myself adopting both sets of expectations, lacking a true sense of my own desires. This marked the beginning of my people-pleasing nature.

In an attempt to meet these expectations, I not only learned how to cook but I also rebelled in my own way, through my unique culinary exploration. I ventured beyond the dishes my mother prepared, exploring a wide array of desserts such as chocolate fudge, pies and various cakes. Baking became my passion. I also delved into gourmet recipes from books, creating dishes that were vastly different from my mom's cuisine.

Roti was a staple in our household, served every single day, yet, I never mastered the art of making it myself. Every morning my mom would make roti as part of our breakfast. Strangely, I cannot even say that I made an effort to learn. It seems there has always been an internal barrier preventing me from acquiring the skill of making roti.

That's not to say that I did not emulate my mom. Looking in the rearview mirror, I see that there are many commonalities between myself and my mom. She loved to entertain and so do I. She loves to be well-dressed and groomed and so do I. But I digress....

While at Peacock Hill, I attended a local prep school. One Christmas, either in 1975 or 1976 – memory fails me, I was six or seven years old – I stole a bottle of bubble bath from a child during Christmas pixie gift giving at school. I can't recall why I did such a thing but I did do it. My dad was informed when he came to pick me up.

Needless to say, he was extremely angry and being intolerant of imperfections and wrong doing, I was severely punished. My punishment may seem inhumane. It was; but in hindsight I realize that my dad was simply reacting according to how he had been brought up – in a culture of slavery and indentured servants.

I was bound by my wrists and hung from the eaves of the house. The eave is really just the underside of the roof that projects from the house. So, yes, I was hung from the eaves with no clothes on except for my underwear.

My dad then caned me for periods of time, left, then he would return to cane me some more. I certainly did learn a lesson that evening. I don't remember how I was taken down or by whom. My mom once said that when she returned from work, she saw me hanging and cut me down. I was severely welted and mentally broken.

You might think that this would have been the end of a good relationship with my dad. It was not. I cannot explain it but I still adored my dad. Perhaps, I thought the crime deserved the punishment.

Perhaps, it marked the beginning of my acceptance of abuse by those who say they love me.

To say that I came from a dysfunctional family is putting it mildly. My upbringing unfolded within the confines of a home that was a crucible of challenges. I can vividly recall witnessing physical altercations between my parents. It was a dreadful and frightening experience and it recurred on numerous occasions. As a young child, these scenes of domestic abuse left an indelible mark on my impressionable mind, shaping my perception of relationships and casting a shadow over my understanding of marriage and love.

Within the whirlwind of the chaos that enveloped my world, I sought refuge in the realm of make-believe. In the sanctuary of my daydreams, I wove a narrative where rescue awaited, sparking the fantasy that a knight in shining armor would arrive to liberate me. My fervor for fairy tales knew no bounds – I was captivated by stories of princesses finding their Prince Charming and basking in a life of eternal happiness. This enduring fantasy persisted subconsciously, well into the period leading up to the writing of this book, exerting its influence over my adult relationships.

Now, I stand at a juncture where fresh clarity dawns upon me – the notion of a Prince Charming sweeping me off my feet is but a distant dream. This realization has found its place within me and is warmly embraced. I know that the task of saving myself rests squarely upon my shoulders. Within the narrative of my life, I am both the damsel and the knight, a dual role that paints me as the architect of my own salvation.

From a tender age, reading emerged as a passion of mine, offering a haven where I could escape the perplexities that enveloped my world. I spent hours with *Nancy Drew* and *The Hardy Boys*, which later led to light romance novels and progressed to historical fiction.

Even now, reading remains a part of my life, albeit predominantly non-fiction, though not to the extent of my youth – a shift I attribute to the prevalence of contemporary devices and distractions. Undoubtedly, it all boils down to the allure of diversion. In the past, I turned to reading as a means to veer my thoughts away from the reality surrounding me. Rarely was I fully engaged in the present moment. When

I wasn't immersed in books, I found refuge within the confines of my own imagination.

During my stay at Peacock Hill, two other loves of my lives were born, my brothers Steve and Robert. They were born two years apart and being seven years older than Steve, I began my role as surrogate mom, or at least that's what I told myself.

As my mother focused on caring for newborn Robert, I relished the responsibilities of being a big sister to Steve. The deep love I felt for him awakened my maternal instincts, which have remained with me ever since. This enduring connection to motherhood has become my most cherished passion.

Around the age of nine, my parents acquired a local business situated in Golden Grove, St. Thomas — a petrol station and a snack counter. It was a mere ten-minute drive from our home on Peacock Hill. Both of my parents maintained their jobs on the sugar plantation but this acquisition brought about a significant change in my routine.

My parents devoted a considerable amount of time to the business, and as a result, we, the children, also spent a great deal of time there. I vividly remember observing my father as he diligently pumped petrol and conducted stocktaking, a task that demanded daily attention during those times. I assisted him, cherishing the opportunity to be by his side and contribute in any way I could.

However, there were challenges. My father struggled with excessive drinking, introducing another layer of dysfunction into our lives. In fact, I am convinced that he battled alcoholism. During school breaks, we, as children, would reluctantly accompany him as he frequented various rum bars. Even so, it was during moments of sobriety that he would impart valuable wisdom to me, emphasizing the immeasurable worth of education.

He introduced me to the different levels of tertiary education, including the seemingly unattainable PhD degree. His dream for me was to become a medical doctor, and naturally, it became my dream as well.

My father's resolute focus on education was truly remarkable. Even though he had limited formal education himself, only completing primary school due to financial constraints, he possessed an astonishing brilliance and an innate ability to learn quickly. His determination to excel in life, coupled with his thirst for knowledge, served as an inspiring example to me and left an indelible mark.

Dad was also a philanderer, and would take me on 'dates' with other women. He had an eye for the young girls and was quite blatantly an adulterer. I marvel at the fact that my mother put up with that behaviour, but again it seemed I emulated her in my own marriage.

I also acquired valuable lessons from my father regarding the significance of money and the art of saving. Throughout his life, he consistently prioritized saving for the future, instilling in me the principles of financial management and budgeting from an early age. At the same time, he was always generous to his children ensuring that we were never in a state of need.

Conversely, my relationship with my mother was characterized by stormy interactions. Although she did not resort to extreme physical punishment like binding or caning, she frequently resorted to slapping and shouting at me. It became a distressing part of my daily life. There were stretches of time when my mother and I would go without speaking to each other, creating an atmosphere of silence and tension.

The silent treatment, especially when experienced from one's own mother, can be an incredibly painful and bewildering experience. It is a form of emotional manipulation and control where communication and connection are intentionally withheld. It is particularly damaging, as it reinforces a sense of unworthiness and rejection. Growing up with this pattern of behavior has left deep emotional scars, impacting my self-esteem and ability to form healthy relationships.

These experiences have contributed to my heightened sensitivity and strong reactions to being given the silent treatment by loved ones in my adult life. Even now, I find myself deeply affected by the experience of being ignored or shut out by people I care about. When faced with the silent treatment in relationships, the echoes of that childhood pain resurface, triggering feelings of abandonment and anxiety. It serves as a reminder to prioritize open communication and strive for healthier ways to address conflicts in my relationships.

The prevalence of dysfunction within families is a painful reality, often yielding repercussions on the mental and emotional well-being of children. In the midst of an environment rife with emotional abuse, neglect, or ceaseless discord, young minds can internalize damaging self-perceptions, nurturing seeds of low self-esteem. Gradually, a distorted image takes shape – a belief in their own inadequacy, an unworthiness of love, attention, or recognition. Regrettably, these misconceptions may persist into adulthood.

Additionally, dysfunctional family dynamics often breed codependent relationships, where children are conditioned to prioritize the needs of others over their own. This codependence can make individuals vulnerable to developing unhealthy attachments and struggling to establish boundaries in their relationships.

The accumulation of these negative experiences and distorted beliefs can contribute to a heightened risk of suicidal ideation as a means to escape pain.

This was the case with me. Throughout my life, even as a child, I have carried the weight of suicidal ideation to varying degrees. It seems as though it has always been a part of me, ingrained in the very essence of my being. Perhaps, I was born with it, or perhaps it was a product of my tumultuous experiences.

There was always that emptiness, that persistent void in my heart that would occasionally dissipate, granting me fleeting moments of respite. But more often than not, it lingered as a haunting presence, an ever-present back drop to my existence. It was a darkness in my soul. My soul was crying out for God, only I did not know this.

My suicidal ideation and that hole in my heart compelled me to seek answers in the offices of psychologists, psychiatrists, counsellors and even Christian healers. This quest began when I was just twenty-four years old, but the troubles that led me there had plagued me for many years prior. While my husband was aware of my mental health challenges, I felt that he did not invest enough time or effort in truly comprehending the medical roots of these issues. His lack of genuine interest in my mental health only added to the sense of isolation and frustration I felt while grappling with these challenges. I did not feel supported.

I longed to unravel the enigma of my inner emptiness and catch a fleeting glimpse of the elusive happiness that remained seemingly out of grasp. I constantly looked to others for happiness and validation, including my husband. I was unaware that its true essence lay within me all along.

Those of us who contend with suicidal thoughts, myself included, are not just abstract concepts. We come in various forms – possessing degrees, displaying attractiveness, exuding charisma, leading organizations, even gracing television screens. We garner respect, and we might even be individuals you would envy. Yet, beneath these external layers, our cores bear silent suffering. Sadly, recent times have witnessed far too many notable figures, both male and female, succumbing to the tragic grip of suicide.

Dysfunction is pervasive. It is not an anomaly; it is prevalent in nearly every household, taking diverse forms. As *Homo sapiens*, we all exist on the spectrum of dysfunction. Each of us carries distinct experiences, obstacles, and flaws, and we each have differing thresholds for handling dysfunction.

Understanding and accepting this concept can be difficult for individuals who perceive themselves as "normal" or unaffected by dysfunction. People may be quick to judge and say things like, "I went through worse, but I still love life. I am not feeling suicidal." While it may be true for some individuals, it is crucial not to rush to judgment or dismiss the struggles of others.

Mental illness is a real and genuine battle that many face.

CHAPTER 4

School Challenges

At the tender age of ten, I faced a pivotal moment in my academic path – the Common Entrance exam – an entrance examination into high school that carried the weight of determining my educational trajectory. The pressure to excel weighed heavily upon me, as the stakes were high. I was nervous about the exam, as it was important to do well in order to avoid repeating a year in school.

Before the exam, parents were asked to rank their top three choices for high schools. My parents' first choice was a boarding school located in another parish some distance away. No student from my school had ever been accepted to their first choice if it was out of parish. My parent's second choice was located in the parish.

The day of reckoning arrived as the examination results were published in the national newspaper. Anxiously, I awaited news of my performance, while my father ventured on an early morning mission to obtain the newspaper. He assured me that if I had passed, the triumphant blare of his vehicle's horn would resonate as he approached our home. But as the minutes ticked by, and the sound of the horn eluded my ears, panic began to consume me. I heard when my dad drove into the driveway and believing I had failed, I sought refuge in the bathroom, trembling with fear.

A few minutes later, I heard my father calling my name. I emerged from my hiding place, ready to face the disappointment and disapproval of my father, only to discover that I had indeed triumphed in the exam and secured a place at the coveted boarding school. The news was an unprecedented achievement, igniting a wave of delight and celebration. My father had been so excited that he had forgotten to honk the horn. This was a momentous occasion for me and my family. It was the first time that a student from my school had been accepted to a boarding school.

Nonetheless, my elation at my venture into the realm of boarding school proved to be a fleeting one. Despite having a close friend who also attended this school, albeit in a higher grade, an unexpected and overwhelming wave of homesickness and grief crashed upon me. The yearning for familiarity, even with all its dysfunction, became an insurmountable burden, and tears flowed endlessly.

Recognizing my distress, my parents intervened and orchestrated a transfer to a school nestled in the neighboring parish of Portland, where I would have the opportunity to commute on a daily basis. I was much happier at this new school.

Human nature tends to gravitate towards the familiar, for even when it's uncomfortable, it can provide a sense of security compared to the unpredictability of change. Moreover, the decision to stay put may be laced with underlying fears such as the fear of stepping into the unknown or the fear of relinquishing the little stability one has. This psychological concept is often termed the 'comfort zone,' a space in which individuals tend to linger despite the discomfort, just to remain within the bounds of familiarity.

This occurs in all different types of relationships, whether it be a toxic friendship, a dysfunctional family dynamic, or a problematic work environment. The bonds formed over time, no matter how detrimental they may be, can create a sense of loyalty and attachment that make breaking free from such situations incredibly challenging.

When I was twelve years old, a year after my transfer to this new school in Portland, my parents purchased a beautiful home in Morant Bay, St. Thomas that stands as our cherished family abode to this day. This move not only marked the beginning of a new chapter but also necessitated another change in my life's trajectory. With our roots now firmly planted in Morant Bay, it became apparent that attending the high school in Portland would no longer be feasible. Thus, I began a new course, transitioning to a different high school that aligned with our new location. My sojourn at the high school in Portland lasted only one and half years.

Embarking on a new chapter in my educational journey, I enrolled at Morant Bay High School, setting foot into its halls during the beginning of the second term of second form, equivalent to grade eight. As an unfamiliar face in this new environment, trepidation coursed through my veins. Shyness gripped me, and the fact that I stood out as one of the few students of Indian descent only added to my self-consciousness. It was in this very school that my now ex-husband had also pursued his education, intertwining our paths in unexpected ways.

Morant Bay High School presented me with a unique challenge as they conducted their internal examinations in January, just as I arrived as a newcomer. This meant diving headfirst into unfamiliar territory, including the subject of French that was entirely new to me.

Additionally, I encountered content in subjects such as Social Studies that I had never encountered before. Notwithstanding the daunting nature of the situation, I had no choice but to face the exams. The examination results though anticipated, were discouraging – I ranked 36th out of 40 students in my class.

Thankfully, my parents empathized with my predicament, understanding the difficulties I faced during this transitional period. Nevertheless, some of the teachers lacked the same level of understanding. Previously accustomed to securing top positions in my classes, this experience of failure was entirely new and disheartening.

The pressure intensified as my father, placing immense importance on my academic achievements, expected nothing less than excellence. Additionally, I distinctly remember my Social Studies teacher uttering discouraging words, proclaiming that I would never excel in the subject. Little did she know, her remark served as fuel to ignite my motivation and determination.

With a firm resolve to prove her wrong, I set out on a course of study and dedication. I resolved to push through the challenges.

When the June examinations arrived, I seized the opportunity to demonstrate my capabilities. I emerged as the top student in my class, securing the coveted first place in Social Studies, and if my memory serves me right, securing second place in French.

Once again, I reclaimed my status as a top-performing student, and the sense of pride that radiated from my father affirmed my accomplishments. In fact, he had a unique way of acknowledging my accomplishments by rewarding me financially for each first-place achievement (though I must clarify that I do not endorse or recommend this practice to other parents).

At the time when I attended Morant Bay High School, the institution grappled with a significant shortage of competent teachers and lacked the necessary resources to adequately support quality education. This dismal reality made my academic journey that much more challenging.

From a young age, as mentioned before, I harbored aspirations of becoming a medical doctor – a dream heavily influenced by my father's desires for my future. As I progressed through my schooling, I steered my academic focus towards science subjects paving the way for my intended career goal.

My ambitions were later dampened during my time in fifth form (grade 11), a critical year in my academic pursuits. It was during this period that another incident occurred leaving an enduring mark on my spirit. I have made efforts to forgive but I remain uncertain if I have fully been able to do so. The event, shattered the very core of my being leaving behind deep emotional wounds.

The catalyst for this profound impact was my male Physics teacher – a figure of authority who wielded significant influence over the young minds entrusted to his care. He had asked students to return to school during the Christmas break to catch up on some laboratory work. This teacher made inappropriate physical advances towards me in the laboratory preparation room. As a sheltered and naïve fourteen-year-old, this left me traumatized and ashamed. I was distraught. He destroyed my sense of trust and security, violating the boundaries that should have been respected.

I always sat at the front of the class and the teacher continued to deliberately pass his hands across my bosom during classes. I would literally tremble and visibly shake before going into his class. This led to a complete and total mental block to Physics. I failed Physics at GCE O' Level and had to repeat this subject the following year. I was totally unable to learn in his class.

While some may consider what happened to me to be a minor infraction, the impact on my life has been great. It influenced my parenting skills as I became an over protective mom determined that my children not experience such an incident.

Even to this day, a lingering resentment towards the school persists within me for their failure to detect and address the problem I faced. I acknowledge that I kept silent, choosing not to confide in my parents or anyone else – an unfortunate tendency often exhibited by victims. Reflecting on this, I struggle to comprehend why I made that choice, but it is an all-too-common characteristic of those who have suffered such abuse.

What perplexes me the most is the fact that even though I was a top student, excelling in all subjects, my decline in Physics went unnoticed. It was as if no one discerned the glaring disparity between my performance in that particular subject and my achievements in all the other subjects. I am saddened by the absence of investigation and intervention.

I wish that there had been conscientious adults with the good sense to inquire and to intervene. It is unfortunate that occurrences like mine, and even more distressing incidents are all too common within our education system.

On the day of my Physics exam, after completion and being fully aware of my imminent failure, I confided in my mother. The details of what transpired afterward remain locked away in the recesses of my mind, shielded by the protective mechanism of repression. I do not believe much was ever done about this monster that called himself a teacher.

Although I had experienced a setback in Physics, I was the top performer and was bestowed the honor of being the Valedictorian for that year – an anxiety-inducing experience, given my lack of public speaking prowess. I also proceeded to take on the role of Deputy Head Girl.

The scars left by that teacher's actions remain with me to this day. As I recount this painful incident, my heart races and distress washes over me. Regrettably, I am also filled with an intense anger towards this monster who stole a child's innocence.

It is my fervent hope that collectively we can forge a path towards establishing an environment where students are shielded from such abuses fostering a future of well-being in their lives.

The scars remain.

CHAPTER 5

My Eyes Deceive Me

I am now twenty-four years old and the loneliness of my two-year marriage gave birth to my desire to have a child.

With my husband juggling his demanding work schedule and his dedication to his studies, he found himself away from home more often than not. While I deeply appreciated his efforts to support us, the lack of companionship took its toll, and I longed for someone to share an emotional connection with.

I tried my best to understand his commitments and supported his aspirations, but I could not shake the feeling of being adrift without a confidant by my side. Notwithstanding, I knew that his hard work was motivated by his desire to provide both of us with a better future.

As the latter half of 1993 unfolded, a longing welled up within me – an intense yearning to bring a child into the world. This desire, born from a combination of factors, was fueled by a potent mix of loneliness that had infiltrated my marriage and a persistent void that gnawed at the core of my being. It was as if an invisible emptiness echoed through the chambers of my heart, urging me to commence the transformative journey of motherhood.

My eagerness to start a family coincided with the time that my scientific research had ended and I was faced with the arduous task of crafting my PhD thesis. As the call of motherhood whispered to me, I discussed my wish with my husband, who agreed. With a mixture of anticipation and trepidation, I embarked on the necessary gynecological checks and eagerly embraced the journey toward conception.

It was not until April 1994, amid the aftermath of a harrowing car accident involving my husband at the wheel and a motorcyclist, that the news of my long-awaited pregnancy arrived. A wave of joy washed over me as I savored the knowledge that a precious life was growing within. Still, alongside the elation, the pregnancy proved to be taxing. Throughout the months, I suffered with bouts of twenty-four-hour morning sickness, leaving me physically drained though filled with anticipation.

I was not the only one eagerly awaiting this

precious addition to our family. My parents and brothers shared in the excitement, thrilled to welcome the first child of a new generation into our lives.

An early ultrasound revealed the wonderful news that a baby boy was growing within my womb. In celebration of this precious life, my parents organized a traditional East Indian ceremony, dedicated to protecting and blessing the little one growing inside me. The ceremony took place at my family home, where the warmth of our traditions enveloped us all. Both my husband and I played integral roles in this event, embracing my cultural heritage and sharing in the love and prayers for our soon-to-be-born son.

On the memorable day in December 1994, my world was forever transformed as my cherished son, entered this world through a caesarian section. In that transformative moment, the threads of my existence rewove themselves, creating a fabric of unconditional love and joy. The arrival of this precious life breathed new meaning into every aspect of my being, setting me on a path that would forever alter the course of my life as a woman and a mother.

From that day onwards, I poured my heart and soul into child rearing. It blinded me to many of the wrongs that took place in my marriage.

I put the marriage on the side burner and put my son first. In hindsight, I see how wrong this was. *One should never make a child the centre of one's universe.*

It came back to bite me in later years.

Nothing prepares you for the challenges of parenting. While there were many joyous moments, the agony of child illnesses and sleepless nights were devastating for me. My husband did his best to help and support me during these early years. His love for our son was undeniable, and he fully committed to fatherhood, playing his role with dedication and care.

When my son was just a few weeks old my husband had to go away for three weeks to do work in a foreign country. It was a difficult period as there were no cellular phones in Jamaica at that time and my communication with my husband was limited. Being alone with a newborn baby intensified the emotional weight of his absence. It was during those trying days that my brothers stepped up as devoted uncles, visiting frequently to offer a helping hand and bringing some much-needed light to my days.

My son, well, he was quite the handful, yet my heart overflowed with affection for him each and every day. His boundless energy and rambunctious spirit kept me on my toes, but I would not have had it any other way. His infectious enthusiasm and curiosity about the world around him filled every corner of our lives with vibrant colors. He had a mischievous streak, and I would often find myself chasing after him as he embarked on adventures around the house and its environs.

When my son was about nine months old, I began my first job at the Scientific Research Council. I still remember my son's eyes as he watched me try on work clothes for the first time. He was so perceptive, he burst into tears even though I was only trying on the work attire. He somehow instinctively knew that I was going to start a job. It was agonizing to leave my son, but we needed the money and I needed to put my degrees to work.

My husband eventually gained employment with a financial institution where travel was not a necessity. With two salaries, we decided to save one person's salary and use the other salary for expenses. We aspired to purchase a home. When my son was about two years old, we purchased our first bungalow style, three-bedroom house with lots of land space.

Even during the purchase of our first home, a moment that should have been filled with excitement, a major issue arose. My husband proposed taking out a cheaper loan under his brother's name. This meant that his brother would be named on the house title, effectively excluding me as an equal owner of our new home. It became evident that even back then, my husband was using his cunning abilities to outsmart and disregard my concerns. I voiced my strong disagreement with this decision but my concerns were ignored, and my husband went ahead with his plan. It felt as though I had relinquished my power and autonomy in the relationship.

This incident was a foreshadowing of the dynamics that would unfold throughout our marriage. It became a pattern where my opinions and wishes were dismissed, leaving me feeling invalidated and powerless. As time went on, it became increasingly clear that my voice was not valued or heard in the decisions that affected both of us as a couple. I realized that my own well-being and happiness had taken a backseat in the relationship.

****

Now, I step back into our newly acquired three-bedroom abode. While the bedrooms were on the smaller side, the ample living space more than made up for it. It allowed us to host lively get-togethers, and the seamless transition between the family room and the outdoors made our home feel even more inviting. One of the standout features of the house was the old-fashioned brick barbecue in the backyard, which quickly became a favorite spot for us.

The kitchen was in dire need of renovation. The existing cabinets had seen better days, so we decided to embrace a fresh, modern look with all-white cabinetry. It was a trend at that time, and it breathed new life into the space, giving it a bright and timeless appeal.

Stepping outside of my new home, I was greeted by an incredible sight. A magnificent eucalyptus tree stood proudly in the centre of the wide lawn, its bluish green leaves dancing in the gentle breeze. Among the various trees in the yard, a delightful mango tree added its charm to the landscape.

However, the outdoor space had become quite overgrown, with parasitic vines entangled around the trees. It took us a considerable amount of time and effort to clean up the area, but the rewards were beyond measure. As the once-tangled greenery was transformed into a peaceful oasis, I could not help but fall in love with my new home.

After a month of renovations and hard work, we finally moved into our new residence. As someone with a flair for design and decor, I relished the process of putting the house together, making it a reflection of my style and personality.

Having grown up in homes with plenty of open land, moving to a place with lush green spaces was a dream come true. I have always cherished spending time outdoors, and now, with this beautiful outdoor area, I felt truly content. Even my parents admired my new home, and I was pleased to host my mother's fiftieth birthday party there.

During this time, I continued to dedicate myself to my new job, where I reconnected with my dear friend Denise who also worked there, someone I knew from my high school days. As colleagues, we found ourselves collaborating on projects and supporting each other professionally, and so a strong friendship developed.

The time spent there proved invaluable, allowing me to gather experiences and insights as I ventured through various departments. Meanwhile, my husband pursued his studies and eventually achieved his goal of becoming a chartered accountant.

To help care for our little one, I had the assistance of a young lady who lived with us, returning to her home every two weeks on weekends. One night, something unsettling occurred. I awoke around 2:00 am and noticed that my husband was not by my side. I started searching for him. His office and my son's room turned up empty, and as I made my way to the back of the house, I heard the faint sound of a television coming from my helper's room.

Her door was locked. This was not a standard door as it did not go right up to the top of the door jam. There was a six-inch gap between the top of her door jam and the upper part of the door itself.

Curiosity and unease led me to climb up and peek through the gap above her door. To my dismay, I saw her sitting on her bed, dressed in her nightgown, while my husband stood next to her bed, holding a wad of tissues.

Although I did not witness their physical intimacy, it was sorely evident to me, what had transpired. How could a married man find himself in his helper's bedroom at such an hour, with the door deliberately locked?

My husband's explanation was that he could not sleep, so he aimlessly wandered until he heard the television in her room and decided to join her. But deep within, I did not believe him. One would have to be a fool to believe such a feeble story. I struggled with the reality of the situation, feeling a mix of hurt, confusion, and anger. It was as if the ground beneath me had shifted, and I began to question the truth and my own judgment.

Looking back, I realize that this was the beginning of gaslighting – a manipulative and narcissistic tactic used to make me doubt my perceptions and experiences. In those vulnerable moments, I allowed doubt to cloud my instincts, questioning whether I was overreacting or misinterpreting the situation.

It is said that narcissistic gaslighting is a form of emotional abuse where the narcissist intentionally manipulates or distorts the truth so that the victim doubts his or herself. It causes you to question your own sanity and to question if you really saw what you saw. Usually, the victim has low self-esteem.

Within the confusion, self-doubt plagued me, clouding my mind. The thought of leaving the marriage lingered in my brain, but fear gripped my heart. The uncertainty of life without my husband loomed over me.

How would I manage the bills?

What about custody of my son?

The thought of a custody battle terrified me. Instinctively, I knew that my husband would stop at nothing to gain control, even if it meant using our son as a pawn to hurt me. In later days this was proven to be true.

I firmly believed that my husband would employ every means at his disposal to gain custody of our son, leaving me feeling apprehensive about my chances in the legal battle. I feared that I would not be able to outmaneuver my husband in court. My son's feelings would simply be an afterthought to him, overshadowed by his desire for control. The thought of such a fight within the courts weighed heavily on my heart, leaving me fearful for my future and that of my son.

With each passing day, I continued to question my ability to stand independently, doubting if I could truly make it on my own. I felt as though I was trapped, convinced that I needed this man in spite of the various forms of abuse I endured. My lack of self-esteem and self-worth kept me tethered, holding me back from finding the strength to break free and navigate my own path.

But that was not all, I had the intense fear of being alone, of being without a partner. This fear has followed me even to this day as I write this chapter. This fear of being alone is powerful. It holds us captive within a crumbling relationship. For me, the thought of facing life without a partner was intense. I still struggle with that demon and I tend to cling to the familiar, even if it means enduring a relationship filled with pain and disappointment.

My judgement was obscured, convincing me that staying in an unhappy marriage was better than being on my own. It was a complex mix of emotions, where the comfort of companionship outweighed the toll it took on my well-being. Ultimately, it was this fear that kept me trapped, unable to break free from the chains of a broken relationship.

I also thought about the embarrassment. I felt ashamed that my marriage could have ended so soon. I grew up in a family that did not believe in divorce even though it was becoming more common at that time. So, I did what I commonly do, I blocked the incident out of my mind, I repressed my emotions and I pretended the incident did not happen.

However, I was uncomfortable with that household helper and despite my husband's protests, I dismissed her. I could not fathom continuing to live with that person... and so the marriage continued framed by the shadow of infidelity.

I grew up in a traditional family and as a result, the roles within my marriage followed a similar pattern. My husband took charge of the finances, while I dedicated myself to managing the home and caring for our son.

At that time, my husband had a stable job and had even started his own private accountancy practice with a small group of clients. Initially, it seemed like a convenient arrangement, as he handled the financial aspect with ease, leaving me to focus on the household and our son.

Yet, the passage of time unveiled the deliberate repercussions woven into that choice. Allowing my husband unfettered dominion over our financial matters amounted to an unwitting relinquishment of a substantial fragment of my self-reliance and self-governance. The lopsided nature of this power dynamic would come to light later, when our relationship began to crumble under the weight of his manipulative behavior and emotional abuse.

In hindsight, I see that it was a critical mistake to solely rely on my husband for financial matters. It made it even more challenging for me to leave the marriage, as I feared the uncertainty of managing finances on my own. I was also unaware of our true financial position and had little knowledge of the whereabouts of all our savings. This dependence on my husband made it harder for me to imagine a life without him.

It is essential for anyone, regardless of their background or upbringing, to recognize the importance of financial independence and mutual respect within a relationship. I have learnt from my experiences and now understand the significance of standing on my own feet, ready to face whatever challenges life may bring.

I urge readers, male or female, to invest in your financial literacy and take steps towards financial independence, regardless of your current circumstances. This involves learning about budgeting, saving, investing, and acquiring necessary skills to manage one's finances effectively.

By taking control of our financial lives, we empower ourselves to break free from unhealthy dependencies and cultivate a future that is built on self-reliance, resilience and personal fulfillment.

Never give up control of finances.

CHAPTER 6

My Heart Stopped

On July 15, 1998, my heart stopped and my life changed forever. The unexpected and untimely death of my father is perhaps the greatest ordeal I have been through to date. On that Wednesday morning, my dad collapsed and died within hours of being rushed to hospital, a suspected heart attack. He was fifty-eight years old. I was crushed and my heart crumbled. I was always a daddy's girl.

I cannot explain the anguish of losing my dad. I mourn him even today. He was always my inspiration and supporter and he left without warning. There were no goodbyes. In fact, three days prior to that fateful day, my mom had thrown him a birthday party. He was born on the 7th of July but the celebration was on the 12th of July. He celebrated with many of his extended family and friends. No one had any clue that this would be the last time they saw him.

My son was three years old at the time, the first and only grandchild my dad would know. I spoke to my dad the very evening before and he was perfectly fine. He even spoke to my son.

The memory of that fateful day in July, remains etched in my mind with vivid clarity, as if the sands of time had stood still. It was a day when the tranquility of my world was shattered, forever altering the course of my life. Indeed, even now, as I trace the map of my life, I mentally segregate it into two distinct periods: the time before my father's passing and the time that followed.

At the time of this tragedy, my brother Robert resided with me while my other brother Steve was at home in St. Thomas with my parents. My mom called at about 5:00 am to say my dad got up to use the bathroom and had collapsed and that they were at the local hospital. Panic gripped my heart, constricting my breath, as I clung to the fragile awareness that he remained among the living. He was still alive!

In that frantic and heart-wrenching moment, a race against time began. We made a flurry of calls, desperately seeking an air ambulance that could transport my father to the specialized care he needed at the major hospital in Kingston.

My brother Robert and I then embarked on the arduous trip, our hearts heavy with worry and apprehension, as we made our way to the hospital in St. Thomas. One third of the drive in, my mom called to say that an air ambulance had being arranged to air lift my dad to the hospital in Kingston and so there was no point in continuing the journey. We were to turn back and await my dad's arrival in Kingston.

Then the unimaginable, the unexplainable, the unjust, the unacceptable, the cruelest experience happened. At around 7:00 am, the phone rang and I answered. It was an unknown voice. She identified herself as a nurse at the hospital where my dad was. The unbearable truth hung heavy in the air, as my mother's cries of grief reverberated in the background. Through her sobs, she uttered the words, "Just tell her, just tell her". The truth was undeniable, devastating in its finality. My dad had passed. My father had slipped away from us, leaving behind an unfathomable void.

In that moment, our world crumbled around us. The weight of loss bore down upon our shoulders, threatening to consume us entirely. I screamed out my brother Robert's name, and he came rushing to my side. He saw my face, and in that instance he knew. The anguish in our eyes mirrored each other's pain, as we hugged each other, seeking consolation in our shared grief. My husband, who was in the shower at the time, emerged and offered his support.

As my husband resumed his work obligations, Robert and I embarked once again on the drive back to St. Thomas, one marked by heartache, disbelief and sorrow.

As we drew nearer to the hospital, we came upon the hearse transporting my dad's lifeless body to the funeral home. We altered our course and trailed closely behind; our hearts heavy with grief. On arrival at the funeral home, we watched as my dad's body was removed, but as they lifted him up, a guttural sound came from his body tearing through the silence.

My heart shattered into a million fragments, and I cried out in desperate denial, proclaiming that he was not dead. But reality pierced through the haze of anguish. I was gently reminded that the sound I had heard was a mere exhalation of air, a final release from his mortal vessel.

The truth engulfed me like a tidal wave. My beloved father, the pillar of strength and love in my life, had truly departed from this world. No amount of yearning or wishful thinking could alter the devastating truth. He was indeed dead. My beloved father was gone.

I owe my dad so much but in particular I owe him my education as previously mentioned. Even though he was not formally uneducated, he was brilliant. He wanted all of his children to be educated and would always speak to me about university and the various degrees one could attain. He encouraged me to study and to excel. He wanted me to become a medical doctor. My path did not take me there but he was happy with the doctorate degree. My father's primary desire was to see the 'DR' before my name. I believe he hoped this would encourage me to retain my maiden name, even after marriage.

I spent more time with my dad than my mom due to the fact that his job took him in the field and I was able to accompany him during my school breaks as he worked. My mom had a more rigid office job. While I was pursuing my Bachelor's degree and resided at the University, dad would visit almost every week irrespective of the one-and-a-half-hour drive. We would go for meals together as well as we went shopping. He was generous and I wanted for nothing.

The funeral of my father was a bitter experience, marked by the convergence of two distinct traditions that shaped his life and our family's heritage. Firstly, we gathered to honor him with a traditional Indian ceremony, steeped in ancient rituals and customs that spoke to the depth of our cultural roots. In the middle of this ceremony, a powerful wave of emotion threatened to engulf me. But then, as if guided by an unseen force, a shift occurred. In that moment, a serene calm washed over me, and I felt an undeniable presence – my father's spirit – enveloping me with love and solace. I felt my father's essence, his spirit reaching out to console me in my darkest hour. It defied explanation, transcending the boundaries of the tangible world. In that ethereal connection, a sense of peace washed over me.

It was as if he had found a way to reach out from beyond the realms of the physical world, assuring me that he was still with me, albeit in a different form. The supernatural encounter defied rational explanation, yet its impact on my heart and soul was undeniable. It was a reminder that love transcends all realms, and the presence of those we hold dear lingers on, even when they depart this earthly existence.

In the days that preceded the funeral, as I lay in bed consumed by grief, it was my son, who became my rock, my source of solace in the darkest of moments. In his tender embrace, he offered a wordless understanding, a comforting presence that eased the weight of sorrow upon my shoulders. With each whispered "Hush mom, hush," he imparted a gentle reminder that even through the unfathomable pain, there was still room for healing and the strength to carry on.

The loss of my father left me grappling with an indescribable void, a chasm of pain that seemed insurmountable. There was no guidebook for navigating this labyrinth of grief, no set track to follow in the wake of such a loss.

As the weight of twenty-five years since his death settles upon my heart, I am often consumed by contemplation, wondering how my father would perceive the person I have become. I wrestle with the haunting question of how he would perceive my vulnerabilities and the mistakes I have made, particularly in the darkest moments when I questioned the value of my own existence.

Have I let him down?

Does he understand the pain that led me to the brink of suicide or the darkness that veiled my spirit?

Or does he gaze upon me from above with a sense of pride, witnessing the strength and resilience that emerged from this darkness?

In moments of quiet reflection, I wish for his guiding presence. I seek solace in the knowledge that the love we shared transcends time and space, forever etched in the tapestry of my being.

The sudden departure of a loved one leaves a lasting mark on the heart, a storm of emotions that words fail to capture. In the depths of my grief, a seed of hope began to take root. It whispered of the possibility of new beginnings, urging me to contemplate the idea of bringing another life into the world. The thought of second child began to take shape, a glimmer of light within the darkness. It was a fragile thread of hope. I discussed my desire to have a second child with my husband, and he agreed.

In September 1998, the miraculous gift of new life blossomed within me once again. With eager anticipation, I looked forward to the new adventure, envisioning the possibility of welcoming a daughter into this world, a beacon of light.

May 1999, heralded the arrival of my precious daughter into this world. Her arrival was nothing short of a blessing that filled my heart to the brim. From the very moment she graced my life, her radiant presence illuminated every corner of my existence. My daughter became a symbol of love, hope, and joy, infusing my days with a sense of purpose and fulfillment that I never thought possible.

The arrival of my second child marked the beginning of a new phase in my life, as I embraced the role of motherhood, now responsible for two beautiful children. Amidst the challenging times of grieving the loss of my dad and navigating a marriage devoid of its former luster, I found purpose in my devotion to my children. They became my anchor.

There was a noticeable contrast in the personalities of my daughter and son. While my son readily accepted his father's assistance, my daughter seemed to prefer only my presence and refused help from anyone else. This created additional demands on me, especially as I recovered from another caesarian section. She was incredibly clingy and attached to me, which, despite the challenges, filled my heart with immense love and joy. Even with the added responsibilities, I cherished the close bond we shared, knowing that our connection was a priceless gift meant to be treasured.

From day one, my son was an adoring and protective big brother. Actually, from the moment I knew I was pregnant, he took ownership of the baby I carried. I recall my son telling persons that he and mommy were having a baby. His innocence was quite amusing.

Although there was a four-year age gap between them, their bond remained strong as they grew up together. It was truly fascinating to witness the strength of their connection. They shared a remarkable closeness, never engaging in fights and always watching out for each other, even in their later years as teens and adults.

Parenting a girl is very different from parenting a boy. There were striking differences. My daughter possessed a gentle nature and lacked the boisterous energy of her brother. She exuded a sense of calmness and was distinctively her own person. While my son had difficulties with breast feeding, my daughter solely preferred breast milk.

Motherhood brought me immense joy, and I whole-heartedly invested myself in my children's upbringing. However, in doing so I neglected my own well-being, prioritizing their needs above my own. I now realize the importance of finding a balance. My personal growth and fulfilment should not have been neglected.

While on my maternity leave as I carried my daughter in my womb, I decided to make a career change. I wanted to be more flexible so that I could spend more time with my two angels. I resigned from my job and instead of full-time employment, I took a part-time lecturing position at a local university. I started by teaching microbiology to pharmacy students. Over time I taught other courses and my class sizes became much larger.

At that time, I was still a very shy and introverted person and I found it quite nerve racking to teach the large groups of two hundred plus students. Eventually, my nerves settled and I became a seasoned lecturer. I had a good friend at that institution who offered much needed guidance and served as a mentor as I embarked on this new chapter.

I took genuine delight in my new role as an educator. Sharing knowledge and facilitating learning brought me immense satisfaction and a sense of fulfillment. During my tenure at the university, I was given the opportunity to pursue a post-graduate degree in adult education. It was difficult resuming the character of student and the resumption of studying, homework and projects were not welcomed by me. Nonetheless, I persevered and I completed the program.

Whilst learning and teaching, I looked forward to being home with my children. I am a creature of habit and so I created rituals for spending time with them. One such ritual was going to our swing set with my daughter and swinging and chatting with her. She absolutely enjoyed this.

When my daughter was around two years old, my husband's mom came to live with us for a period of time. She helped with both children but she had her own illness to deal with. After about two years, she left to another country to live with her other children.

My husband was the sibling that offered the most support both physically and financially to his mom. In my opinion, based on observation, the other siblings did not care that much. I am still amazed by the loyalty that my husband showed to his mom while at the same time facilitating the disloyalty of my own children towards me that would later occur.

Admirably, my husband stood by his mother's side, showing care and support even during challenging times, and even when she did not fully acknowledge his efforts. His devotion to her was resolute, and as an observer, I could not help but recognize him as a dutiful and committed son.

As my workload increased, the need for suitable child care also increased. At some point we got a lady originally from Guyana to assist us. You may recall my previous experience with one particular young lady. Since then, I was always suspicious of the interactions of care givers with my husband. This new lady was an excellent cook and seemed to get along famously with my two children. But I noticed and I felt an undercurrent between my husband and her.

Though I never witnessed anything overtly unusual, I could not help but notice the numerous peculiar allowances my husband made for this lady, which deviated from the usual routine. He granted her time off to attend school and encouraged her to engage in activities like jogging and taking additional breaks away from home.

While I am all for supporting someone's educational aspirations, the concessions my husband unilaterally made, without any discussion with me, raised suspicion. It brought to light the power imbalance which existed, with decisions being made without considering my perspective or input. While I remained open to understanding the reasons behind these allowances, the lack of communication and transparency left me feeling uneasy and questioning the dynamics at play.

In my eyes, my husband appeared manipulative, cunning, and deceitful. The lack of trust between us was undeniable.

I did not have a good feeling.

CHAPTER 7

Another World

So, I now transition to the early school years of my children which opened the door to another world. I was fiercely protective of my children and wanted them to go to a school with a comprehensive curriculum, excellent facilities and competent teachers.

My husband and I opted for a prestigious private preparatory school with substantial tuition fees for my son to attend. My daughter would later attend the same school. To say it was a different world would be an understatement. Suddenly, I found myself amongst a mix of affluent and influential parents, a stark contrast to my own humble background. This new social circle posed a challenge, as I felt ill-equipped and inexperienced in relating to this elevated echelon of society.

Unlike my own upbringing, where my parents did not engage with the parents of my classmates, I discovered that socializing with the parents of my son's classmates held significant importance. Being a 'country' girl thrust into this unfamiliar territory left me unaware of the social expectations that came with it.

Consequently, my son found himself excluded from birthday parties and other social gatherings that his classmates attended. It is important to mention that my son was one of the few children in the class who was of a mixed racial background. My son felt he had to try harder than others to 'fit in'.

My ignorance did not prepare me for this but driven by my deep love for my son, I resolved to break out of my introverted tendencies and actively engage in socializing. My primary motivation was to support him in his quest to find acceptance and belonging within this new environment.

Recognizing the importance of social integration for both my son and myself, I made a deliberate choice to actively engage with the other parents. To my relief, I discovered that the majority of them were genuinely kind-hearted individuals who warmly welcomed me into their social circle.

There was no valid reason for me to have felt excluded in the first place. In no time, my son began receiving invitations to birthday parties and playdates, signaling his growing acceptance and inclusion among his peers. Witnessing his happiness brought immense joy to my heart, reinforcing the notion that when my son thrived, so did I.

As the primary caregiver, I embraced my role enthusiastically. I diligently dropped off and picked up my children from school, ensuring punctuality was a priority. Taking on various responsibilities, I efficiently ran errands, prepared meals, and became their dedicated chauffeur, ferrying them to their various activities. In addition to my caregiving duties, I poured my creative energy into planning elaborate themed birthday parties for both my son and my daughter. Through these celebrations, I gained a reputation for hosting memorable and entertaining events, further solidifying my presence within this new circle.

With an unabashed love for Christmas, I unreservedly embraced the festive spirit that captivates us all. I was a child at Christmas and enjoyed transforming our home into a magical wonderland, both inside and out. Our family room housed a majestic ten-foot Christmas tree, radiating its splendor and enchantment.

I was the self-appointed resident Santa Claus. I delighted in selecting countless presents that would ignite pure excitement in the hearts of our children. Witnessing their joyous faces on

Christmas morning brought me immeasurable happiness.

During the early years, my husband actively participated in the holiday preparations. Together, we adorned the exterior of our home with twinkling Christmas lights, creating a captivating display for all to admire. While my husband was not directly involved in gift shopping, he generously financed our festive purchases, allowing the magic of Christmas to pervade our home.

It became an annual tradition to transform our abode into a Christmas wonderland, where I, like a child once again, reveled in the beauty and splendor of the season.

As the years passed, I initiated a tradition of hosting grand Christmas Eve parties, complete with breathtaking firework displays that illuminated the night sky. Additionally, we celebrated my son's birthday in style in December, ensuring his special day remained distinct from the Christmas festivities. This deliberate separation allowed us to honor and cherish his individuality and to differentiate his special day from the holiday season. Typically, we would go to my parent's home in St. Thomas, on Christmas Day or Boxing Day for a family dinner.

Our children effortlessly claimed the centre of our universe, captivating both my husband and myself with their wonderful and endearing qualities. They were truly remarkable, embodying goodness and bringing us immeasurable joy.

Notwithstanding the joy of parenthood, we inadvertently neglected our marriage and our own emotional needs. While we formed a tight-knit family unit, our roles as husband and wife grew distant. We unintentionally allowed the emotive connection between husband and wife to wane.

Finding moments of solitude as a couple became a rarity, occurring perhaps once a year, if lucky. Yet, we regularly ventured out as a family, united in creating cherished memories together. Conversations between my husband and myself typically revolved around our children; their well-being and educational pursuits becoming our primary focus.

With my new circle of friends from my children's school, I blossomed into what some might describe as a 'social butterfly'. My commitment to raising my children and my attentiveness to their needs earned me respect and admiration. I actively engaged in school life, taking on the role as a class representative and contributing to a range of fundraising activities for their school.

During that period, my husband's presence at the school or outside events was infrequent, leaving many people unaware of his identity. Soon, I was instrumental in providing my husband with new clientele, even as far as helping him to secure a prestigious Directorship position at a prominent company.

I still remember that day when the owner of this company (a grandfather of one of the children in my son's class) approached me while I waited in the school's lobby area to pick up my son. Unbeknownst to me, he had been observing my interactions and expressed admiration for my mothering skills. He proceeded to ask me what my husband did for a living. I told him and he asked me to relay a message for my husband to call him. This I did, my husband called, and the rest, as they say, is history.

Assisting my husband in securing employment and clients for his private practice was not a novel experience. Prioritizing my family's well-being, I stepped into the role of the primary breadwinner during times of instability, until my husband could regain control.

I actively intervened on his behalf, speaking to influential individuals who played key roles in securing him employment opportunities. On reflection, a particular incident stands out, which brought significant embarrassment. He faced termination at a business where I had personally arranged his job placement. This left me feeling ashamed and disheartened. Despite the challenges, I tried my best to support him, hoping that things would improve in time.

It became apparent that my husband harbored some discomfort toward my new circle of friends. From my perception, he seemed to struggle with feelings of inadequacy. He frequently mentioned instances where he believed certain individuals had disregarded or snubbed him, contrasting it with the positive reception I received. From my perspective, none of these claims held any truth.

As the years went by in Prep school, it became apparent that my son required extra help in his academic subjects. He thrived with greater attention and personalized teaching. Since he did not particularly enjoy reading, I took it upon myself to invest extra time in reading with him daily, recognizing the significance of nurturing his love for reading and assisting him in his educational journey.

My son was full of energy and was mischievous at school from time to time, due largely to his playful nature. Both children also had many extra-curricular activities at school as well as outside of school. Throughout the years, these included activities such as piano, swimming, table tennis, lawn tennis, gymnastics, football and ballet lessons.

The task of transporting the children to and from their various activities primarily fell on me, as we made the decision not to hire a driver. My husband's demanding career left him with little available time to assist with these responsibilities, so I willingly took on the role, ensuring the children's' safe and punctual arrivals and departures.

From school drop-offs to sports practices, music lessons, and extracurricular activities, I carefully orchestrated their schedules to make sure they had the opportunity to explore their passions and talents. As I shuttled them from one place to another, I cherished the moments of bonding in the car, engaging in conversations and using the opportunity for teaching moments where we explored life lessons.

Additionally, I was actively engaged in various school events, accompanying them on field trips, cheering them on during sports days and other sporting events, participating in bake sales, and proudly attending prize-giving ceremonies. My commitment to being present and involved in every aspect of their school life was firm, as I cherished every opportunity to support and be a part of their educational journey.

Still, finding a balance between my work schedule and the demands of my children's routines became increasingly challenging. After thoughtful discussions with my husband, we came to a decision: I would step away from my job to embrace the role of a full-time mother and to assist him in his business.

So, during the hours when the children were at school, I dedicated my time and efforts to supporting my husband in his growing business. This involved collaborating with him on writing proposals, and more frequently, I took on the responsibility of running numerous errands directly related to his business operations. There were also occasions when I served as a consultant to my husband's clients, assisting with special projects. Although I was not financially compensated for these contributions, I did not see it as an issue at the time. After all, my husband and I were a team, and I believed that supporting his aspirations was an essential part of our partnership, or so I thought.

Even so, we were always united in our clear focus on nurturing our children's educational pursuits; our collective aim was to empower them to thrive academically.

I was to be a stay-at-home mom.

CHAPTER 8

Déjà vu

*L*ife has a peculiar way of unfolding, filled with unexpected synchronicities. On the fateful day of September 2004, another life changing event occurred. It started off as an ordinary weekday, with me embarking on my short five-minute drive to pick up my children from school. Back then, I drove a Volvo sedan, and our home lacked an automatic gate, leaving it open during the daytime. Additionally, our garage had no doors to shield it from the outside world.

As I pulled into the garage of my home with my two children, I shifted the car into 'park' and prepared to step out, accompanied by my son and my daughter. It was at that moment that two young men rushed in and approached us, one of them brandishing what appeared to be a firearm. They demanded my handbag, to which I willingly surrendered. Rummaging through its contents, they could not find my cellular phone. They demanded to know where it was and I obliged, looking into the bag and providing them with the small phone that I carried at the time.

My daughter froze and tears streamed down her petrified face. She was five years old, the same age as I was when I experienced the home invasion. My son stood with fear in his eyes and watched. At the same time, the Guyanese helper had come out of the house through the side door to assist with the children. When she saw what was happening, she ran back in the house and closed the door. She then called my husband who was at work at the time. She also notified the security company that had armed the house.

I thought it would be the end of the ordeal once the robbers received the handbag, but alas it was not to be so. The younger robber reached for my hand and dragged me to the back of the house away from my children. He appeared to me to be around sixteen or seventeen years old. With the speed of lightening, he reached under my dress and pulled down my underwear. To say that I was shocked would be minimizing the situation. I did not expect that these robbers were also rapists.

I am not a superstitious person; however, I know what I saw. I saw the face of my deceased Dad suspended in air and it was as if his strength took over and I shrieked to the would-be rapist, "Are you mad!" I scratched at him and began to scream as loud as I could. At the same time, my two children ran to where I was and the young rapist ran away. I now had my underwear crumpled in my hand hidden from my children's view. I did not want them to know what had nearly happened.

I ran around the side of the house with the children shielding them with my body as I thought the robbers would try to shoot us. However, they did not follow and they both ran away. I was let into the house through the back door still clutching my underwear.

My husband arrived shortly after. I recall him asking me many times, "Did they rape you". The answer was "No, he tried, but no, it did not happen". He was furious and on the warpath. He drove off in an attempt to find the robbers. I will say that my husband has always been super protective of his family. I cannot fault him in that regard.

Members of the security company as well as the police came by. I had to give a formal statement to the police. I had scratched the would-be-rapist and I thought the police would have been able to obtain DNA from under my fingernails, but Jamaica was still too antiquated with forensic technology to do so. Instead, a man hunt was begun.

The terror that my children experienced still haunts me today. I never, ever wanted them to be exposed to anything close to what I experienced as a child. I endeavored to provide them with a secure and comfortable environment, perhaps even going overboard in my attempts to shield them from the harsh realities of our world.

Yet, life had a different plan. It was déjà vu.

The very next day, one of the robbers called me on my landline. I assumed they got my number from my identification. All my credit cards, driver's license and other essentials were in the handbag that they had stolen. Shock and disbelief paralyzed me as the voice on the other end offered a half-hearted apology. The exact words elude me now, but it was an apology of sorts. My body's reflexive response to fear kicked in, and I found myself frozen once again, just as I would be in later years when a trusted doctor violated my boundaries.

After getting a hold of myself, my sole focus shifted to helping my children overcome the horrors they had endured. They sought solace in our presence, sleeping in our bedroom. In an effort to restore a sense of normalcy to their lives, both my husband and I personally escorted them to school the very next day. We spoke to their teachers, ensuring they were aware of the traumatic events that had occurred. We believed that maintaining their routine would be in their best interest.

As a creative outlet, I encouraged my daughter to draw a picture for me every day, knowing that her love for art could provide a cathartic release. I recall her drawing a picture of the 'bad' man with someone shooting them. There were also drawings of dogs biting them.

We quickly implemented new security measures. We immediately obtained two German Shepherd dogs and installed an automatic electronic gate opener to keep the gate closed at all times, all measures to improve our personal safety. We also took the children to see a child psychologist. We were both so very concerned about how the ordeal would affect them mentally.

The psychologist assured us that the measures we had already put in place were sufficient to help them move away from the incident.

After this ordeal, I had an intense desire to relocate. I wanted to move away from the insidious memories. I wanted a different home as my current home had now become tainted. My husband was in agreement. We had outgrown that home anyway and wanted a bigger space.

And thus, life pressed forward, though in the process, I sidelined my own emotional well-being, directing my entire focus toward the children's needs. I had overlooked the fact that I, too, had been traumatized by the events, and that I needed to heal from the overwhelming sense of powerlessness and anger I felt towards the criminals. My once-fervent drive to protect my children from harm had been wrested from me, leaving me feeling empty and joyless. My emotions were now distilled solely into the external realm of motherhood's joys.

This incident occurred in the same school year that my son was to take his high school entrance exam, known as GSAT in those days. It became my responsibility to ensure he was adequately prepared, aiming for grades that would secure his acceptance into one of the top high schools.

My son, however, faced challenges with restlessness, and though assessed, he was not diagnosed with ADHD. It was, suggested that he might encounter difficulties in grasping certain mathematical concepts. In my role as his mother, I strived to provide the best support I could for this ten- and then eleven-year-old child and I began to tutor my son in mathematics as well as his other subjects to ensure his readiness for the exam.

I sought to strike a balance between enjoyable experiences and academic pursuits, recognizing his love for football and his abundance of social skills. With his handsomeness, charm, and polite demeanor, my son possessed a remarkable personality that remained unchanged over time.

As fate would have it, my son performed admirably in the exams, at least in my humble opinion. Still, his average fell short of the threshold required for admission into the high school that both my husband and I had set our hearts on.

Upon receiving the news, my husband remained largely silent towards my son, but it was I who bore the full force of his anger. He unleashed a torrent of curses and belittling remarks, directing his frustration towards me. I became the scapegoat, as in his eyes my perceived incompetence was the cause, since we had agreed that I would leave my job to ensure my son's entrance into this specific school. That weekend, tears streamed down my face continuously, as I felt an overwhelming sense of unworthiness. During it all, I fought hard not to transfer this unworthiness onto my son, striving to shield him from my emotional turmoil.

Ultimately, my son remained at the same private school he had been attending, albeit at the high school level. Though circumstances had shifted, my dedication to his education persisted, ensuring that he continued his educational journey with love, support and encouragement.

Upon reflection, I now recognize with great certainty that my children were deeply attuned to the underlying discord within my marriage. It is a testament to the remarkable perceptiveness and sensitivity that children possess, often surpassing our expectations. Despite my best efforts to shield them from the painful realities of my marital struggles, their keen ears and watchful eyes may have caught glimpses of the truth, absorbing fragments of the emotional climate that surrounded us.

This realization dawns upon me with a mix of humility and introspection, underscoring the complex web of emotions that shape our lives and how even the most carefully constructed façade cannot conceal the truth from young hearts.

It is a humbling truth that I had overlooked until now, inviting me to delve deeper into the complexities of their experiences and the impact it has had on their personal development and comprehension, ultimately leading to the eventual estrangement.

This was a truth that I had not perceived at the time.

CHAPTER 9

The Mansion

*T*he quest for a new home marked the beginning of a new chapter in our lives. Our primary objective was to discover a more spacious dwelling, conducive to hosting gatherings and most importantly, we were determined to find a secure community that would ensure the safety and well-being of our family.

Many houses were explored, and numerous offers were made, but none materialized. Our determination persisted, and we eventually stumbled upon an aged house located within a highly coveted neighborhood. The abundance of land space and untapped promise instantly ignited our passion. Nonetheless, it was apparent that this house would demand considerable modifications to align with our vision and preferences.

With great anticipation, we submitted an offer that was accepted, awakening a five-year journey towards transforming this property into our dream home. Recognizing the need for professional guidance, we enlisted the expertise of architect Donald, whose previous work had impressed both my husband and me.

While the property was over three-quarters of an acre, a significant area consisted of a steep slope. To unlock the full potential of the land, we decided to take on the ambitious task of constructing a thirty-foot retaining wall and backfilling the area.

Our vision encompassed not one, but two retaining walls – the first serving as the inner boundary, while the second would form the outer boundary, paving the way for a future tennis court on the lower level.

Donald assumed the responsibility of constructing the retaining walls and designing and producing the blueprints for the remodeling of the existing house. The process of erecting the retaining walls spanned an entire year, and was a far more stressful and expensive venture than we had anticipated.

As the remodeling efforts on the house began, it became evident that the envisioned layout and aesthetic we had in mind would not be attainable within the confines of the existing structure. In light of this realization,

Donald proposed a bold and transformative solution – to demolish the current house and embark on a ground-up construction project.

Accepting this advice, we made the courageous decision to start afresh, allowing our dreams to manifest in the form of a brand-new home. As I was no longer in formal employment, I was given the task of working closely with Donald, in designing the ultimate 'dream home'. And so began my immersion into the realms of architectural design and construction management.

While I possessed no prior experience in these domains, my innate talent for design permitted meaningful contribution to the project. Together, Donald and I commenced on an extraordinary journey, crafting a truly magnificent and unique residence.

The process of building our dream home was not without its fair share of challenges and conflicts with Donald. As of now, to the best of my knowledge, my husband still has an ongoing legal dispute against him. The journey of constructing a house from the ground up proved to be a demanding and stressful experience, filled with drama and discord.

Although the ultimate outcome has been a breathtaking and awe-inspiring home that has even been featured in a magazine, I can confidently say that I would not willingly undertake such a venture again.

Juggling the roles of project manager, interior and exterior designer, and landscaper proved to be an arduous and taxing task. Still, the end result was nothing short of extraordinary – an approximately eleven-thousand-square-foot home boasting an infinity edge pool with jacuzzi that left a lasting impression.

How my husband financed such a project remains a question I cannot answer, as I was never involved in the financial aspects and naïvely refrained from questioning the source of funds, since to my knowledge only a very minute sum of money was borrowed from the bank.

Interestingly, in a rather intriguing parallel to the title arrangement of my first home, the title of our new residence incorporated a 1 per cent ownership share for each of two of my husband's siblings. Consequently, I found myself owning 49 per cent of the house, just shy of an equal 50 per cent share. This deliberate allocation ensured that my husband, along with his two siblings, collectively held a majority stake of 51 per cent in the property. It became apparent to me that my husband had orchestrated this arrangement, much like he had done with our previous home as a strategic move to complicate the division of assets in the event of a divorce.

This premeditated and tactical maneuver reflected his calculated approach to safeguarding his own interests, highlighting the complexities and challenges that lay ahead should our marriage take an unfortunate turn. My husband possessed a sharp cunning and a proactive mindset, evidently anticipating any potential divorce with a shrewd foresight.

Shortly after acquiring the property and during the initial stages of devising plans and drawings for our new home, I began experiencing concerning health issues. Persistent fatigue, unexplained rashes that would turn purple, and joint pain became a daily occurrence. Even though I underwent various medical tests, no definitive diagnosis was made.

Taking matters into my own hands, I conducted research and approached a female doctor friend of mine to test me for lupus – a condition I suspected. The results confirmed my fears: I had *systemic lupus erythematosus*.

From that moment on, my life became intertwined with a cycle of blood tests, visits to the rheumatologist, and a regimen of steroid medication. Lupus, an autoimmune disease, meant that my own immune system mistook my body's cells as foreign invaders and launched an attack against them. Some spiritual healers interpret this illness as a manifestation of self-hatred, a battle where one's own self tries to inflict harm. I believe there is some truth in this as my marriage was unfulfilling and devoid of joy, contributing to feelings of self-discontentment. This led to a decrease in my self-worth, further eroding my already fragile self-esteem.

Throughout the course of my treatment, I gradually dwindled to a mere ninety-four pounds, bearing the physical toll of the disease. Even with my illness, I persevered in fulfilling my duties as a mother while also shouldering the responsibilities of project manager and designer for our new home.

After about four to five years, the disease that had plagued me with its mysterious presence suddenly vanished, just as inexplicably as it had appeared. The blood markers that once signaled its presence were no longer detected, and I was deemed to be in remission. This occurrence was incredibly rare and peculiar – a testament to divine intervention and another instance where God saved my life.

It was not until 2012 that we finally made the move into our magnificent mansion, adorned with imported marble floors and floor-to-ceiling windows. The house was still incomplete when we moved, lacking the finishing touches such as the backyard entertainment area with its pool and jacuzzi. Time was also required to furnish the house and tend to the intricacies of the gardens. The end result was nothing short of spectacular – a sight to behold.

Perhaps this is why my now ex-husband harbored such intense fury, spewed venom and sought vengeance when I made the decision to leave. Who could fathom a woman willingly walking away from such opulence and luxury? It became an immense source of embarrassment for him, a blow to his inflated ego that pierced deep like a dagger.

Managing such a huge property was a colossal undertaking. While we had the convenience of a live-in gardener and occasional assistance from a domestic helper, we opted against hiring a professional landscaping company or an interior decorator. Thus, these tasks fell into my hands. Although time-consuming, I did not mind. Embracing the role of both landscaper and interior decorator, I began the journey of creativity and transformation.

Furthermore, I dedicated a substantial portion of my time to proficiently oversee and manage the property. Simultaneously, I remained steadfast in ensuring the continued academic success of both my children. Guiding them through their studies, extending support and fostering an environment of encouragement remained a top priority.

I was unswervingly committed to nurturing their educational journeys.

CHAPTER 10

A Turn of Events

$\mathcal{I}$n the meantime, as the construction of the mansion was taking place, my daughter remained at the same preparatory school that her brother had attended. There were occasional issues, but in general my daughter did well in school and was an avid reader like I was. When it came to her year for doing the GSAT exam, we knew she was on the path for great achievement.

While many other students in her class did extra lessons in preparation for this exam, we did not do that for my daughter. Just as I had done with her brother before, it fell upon me to guide her through the study and preparation process. The examination consisted of five subjects: Science, Social Studies, Maths, English- (graded on a percentage scale) and then there was Communication Task (marked out of 12).

My daughter's performance was truly outstanding and at the time, was unprecedented at her school. She received remarkable scores, securing two perfect 100 per cent scores, two near-perfect 99 per cent scores and an impressive 11 out of 12 for Communication task. Her achievements were a testament to her innate brilliance.

Top performers in the GSAT examinations were given national awards referred to as government scholarships. There was also a top girl and top boy award. My daughter received a government scholarship and she was overjoyed and I was elated. I always knew her potential was limitless. In fact, the day before she sat the exams, we went shopping as a means of distraction. I even gifted her with a gold pendant for her achievement weeks before the exam results. That was how much I was and still am confident in her God-given intelligence.

Throughout the years, my daughter consistently struggled with exam anxiety, and it became my responsibility to provide reassurance and to keep her calm during those nervous moments. Even though my belief in her abilities, she often doubted herself.

In spite of her remarkable exam results, my husband managed to find a way to belittle and undermine me. He accused me of not dedicating enough time to practicing the communication task paper with my daughter, suggesting that it was my failure that prevented her from achieving a perfect score in all subjects. According to him, had I performed my role more effectively, she would have been crowned the top-ranking girl.

In my view, it did not matter. I thought that my husband's need for perfection was outlandish. I could not have been prouder of my incredible super girl. Her achievements filled me with immense pride and her brother shared in that joy. Her brother was over the moon. He has always been my daughter's biggest cheerleader and staunch supporter. There was never an ounce of jealousy over her successes; he totally embraced them as his own. I am so proud of both of them and their sibling love for each other.

Allow me to digress as I recount another incident that remains etched in my memory, transpiring years later when my daughter had begun her journey in tertiary education. During a crucial multiple-choice exam, she inadvertently circled the answer for the wrong question, causing a disruption in the sequence on the answer sheet. Realizing her mistake later on, she attempted to rectify it but was met with the constraint of time. Naturally, she felt upset by the situation.

My husband, in his characteristic manner, seized upon this innocent mistake and twisted it to serve his own narrative. He insinuated that if I had provided proper guidance to our daughter on how to approach multiple-choice questions, such an error would have been averted.

This tendency to assign blame and find fault in me, even in situations where it was unwarranted, revealed a glaring narcissistic trait within him. It seemed that in my husband's eyes, I could never meet his expectations or do anything right. This pattern extended beyond our daughter's exam incident, as he even found fault with the very home we had built together. He habitually pointed out insignificant and often imperceptible flaws in the construction of our home, often placing blame on me for these perceived shortcomings.

My husband's constant inclination to find fault in me left a void within my being, a space that longed to be filled with acceptance and validation. The weight of his criticisms and constant disapproval eroded my self-esteem. I believe that this is what contributed to my vulnerability. I yearned for someone who could appreciate me for who I truly was, someone who could counteract the self-doubt and insecurities my husband's behavior had inflicted upon me. I craved the validation that would affirm my worth and restore my sense of self.

Now, let me refocus our attention back to the subject at play. My daughter was now on her way to the High school we had hoped for her to attend.

As the hand of God continued to guide my life, an opportunity arose for me to visit this new school and have a private meeting with the principal before the new school year began. During our conversation, the principal brought to my attention that they needed a temporary replacement for a science teacher for one school term while the current teacher was on vacation leave.

It is truly beyond words to capture the magnificence of God's ways and the mysterious workings of divine intervention. As if orchestrated by a higher power, a remarkable sequence of events unfolded, leading to a decision that I would step in as the substitute teacher for that particular period. Simultaneously, the school generously considered accepting my son into tenth grade, while my daughter commenced her seventh-grade journey.

The school welcomed my son with open arms, and this new environment had a positive impact on him. He forged new friendships with peers who were both socially engaged and driven academically. This circle of influence inspired my son to do well in his subsequent examinations, ultimately paving the way for him to pursue a career in law and to become an attorney.

So it was that both my children embarked on a new chapter together at this new school and with their mom being there as well. It was an entirely different experience for them, transitioning from the realm of expensive private education to a more diverse and inclusive environment. My presence at their new school during their transition added comfort, familiarity and ease.

The experience of serving as a teacher at this school proved to be both immensely challenging and utterly exhausting. The workload was demanding as I found myself tasked with teaching ten different groups of classes, including my own daughter's class. Balancing the preparation of lesson plans, tests, and worksheets alongside the overseeing of a new home construction project became a juggling act of epic proportions. Nonetheless, within this whirlwind, a new advventure had begun, brimming with opportunities and unforeseen twists.

The wonderful news is that both my children flourished and exceeded expectations at their new school. Words fail to capture the immense pride I feel for both of them. Their achievements and growth serve as a constant source of joy and admiration.

God was shifting my life's story.

CHAPTER 11

Darkness and Then Light

Through the process of constructing my new home, and guiding my children's academic pursuits, I found myself once again consumed by darkness and in the midst of turmoil with my husband. There were moments when he weaponized his words, and they became darts aimed at my heart.

During one particular occasion, overwhelmed by a barrage of disparaging remarks which had become increasingly common, I was engulfed by an overwhelming sense of hopelessness. In a moment of impulsive desperation, I ingested a substantial quantity of prescription sleeping pills that had been prescribed to alleviate my chronic insomnia. It was an act born out of anguish, not premeditation, and it unfolded in the presence of my husband. He did try to stop me swallowing those pills, but I was swift in my actions and swallowed the pills before he could stop me. This was my first suicide attempt.

The sequence of events that followed is somewhat fragmented in my memory, but I do recall my husband's immediate response. With a mix of concern and urgency, he ushered me into his car and raced me to the hospital. The details of that experience remain blurred, but the vivid recollection of medical professionals swiftly attending to me, administering treatments to flush the toxins from my system, lingers in my consciousness.

I also remember a young trainee doctor posing a series of predetermined questions, one of which concerned my highest level of education. On hearing that I held a PhD degree, I remember her remarking, "then why would she want to kill herself". This statement exposed the tremendous ignorance that still exists among many professionals regarding the complexities of suicide and suicidal thoughts.

Suicide and suicidal thoughts are not limited to the less privileged or less educated persons. They transcend social status and wealth. These thoughts are birthed from relationships. Relationship with oneself, relationship with God and relationships with others. Neither do persons attempt suicide to gain attention, it is done because the pain has become excruciating and unbearable.

I recall that it wasn't until about 3:00 am that I was taken over to the private hospital ward for further treatment. My husband remained by my side, displaying genuine concern.

Before, this occasion, I had periodically thought of suicide during the course of the marriage. Suicidal ideation was always part of my psyche. As much as I loved my children, I found that there were times when I simply wanted to be free of the pain and emptiness that consumed me. This emotional fog obscured my rationality, leading me to mistakenly believe that those who cherished me would find greater contentment should I depart from this world.

I am aware that suicidal thoughts can be seen as selfish, and I acknowledge this truth. It is important to understand that these thoughts arise from a sense of hopelessness, extreme mental pain and anguish. It is challenging to articulate the depth of suffering one must endure to reach the point of contemplating ending one's own life. Suicidal ideation is not meant to hurt others, rather, it is seen as an escape from unrelenting suffering.

The sense of fulfillment and emotional connection I craved was conspicuously absent within my marriage, resulting in an underwhelming and lackluster union. When these essential elements are lacking, it can result in a lifeless marital experience. My heart craved emotional connection, a genuine outpouring of affection, and the nurturing companionship of an equal. I hungered to bridge the void within my soul and mend the lingering emptiness that had taken root within me.

That morning waking up in the hospital, I discovered that my husband had informed my children that I had taken ill but that I was ok. He attributed my illness and hospitalization to Lupus, shielding them from the distasteful and harsh reality. I concurred with this decision as they were too young to understand the gravity of my depression. My brothers were notified and offered their support to the best of their abilities, stepping in during this challenging time.

My recovery from my first suicide attempt in 2010, included mandatory psychiatrist visits and medication. I also sought cognitive behaviour therapy (CBT) from a trained professional.

Through the years, I have come to realize that medication alone is not the panacea for my healing. While I recognize that medication can be beneficial for some individuals, it did not help me. From my personal experience and my own research, I firmly believe that the root causes of depression and suicidal ideation are far more convoluted, involving a combination of neurotransmitter imbalances, brain changes, complex trauma, lack of loving relationships and lack of effective coping mechanisms.

Mental illness is an undeniable reality, and the trauma experienced during one's formative years can leave lasting effects. This trauma has the potential to reshape the development of the brain, resulting in long-term repercussions. To effectively cope with past trauma and the subsequent triggers and reactions, the presence of a loving family and supportive partner becomes imperative.

As I engaged in CBT sessions, I delved deeper into exploring my own schemas - patterns of thought or behavior that are considered unhelpful to an individual. It became evident that my two maladaptive schemas were rooted in the fear of rejection and the fear of abandonment.

These schemas influenced the way I interpreted information and shaped my self-perception. Moreover, these beliefs seamlessly intertwined with my persistently low self-esteem, which, even now, remains an ongoing challenge in my personal journey.

Through CBT, I have gained insights into the negative patterns of thinking and behavior that have held me back. I am still working on challenging these maladaptive schemas and on building healthier beliefs and coping mechanisms.

It is important to acknowledge that recovery from mental illness is a multifaceted and complicated struggle. While medication may be a useful tool for some, it is not a one-size-fits-all solution. The complexities of mental health require a comprehensive approach that addresses the underlying causes, the impact of trauma, and the development of healthy coping strategies.

Unfortunately, during my own recuperation, I lacked the support that is crucial in such challenging times, and as a result, my healing process was hindered. I did not have the support of a loving husband; my children were too young and my extended family were kept at a distance at my husband's command.

I found myself continuously grappling with the weight of suicidal thoughts, which, paradoxically became a lifeline, a way for me to convince myself that I held the power to escape the pain by taking my own life. Suicide became a haunting escape plan in my mind that would continue to rear its head later on in my life.

As I continued my recovery, I was searching for ways to calm my mind, relieve my depression and cope with challenges of living with Lupus. It was during that time that I stumbled upon the practice of yoga. I decided to join a popular yoga studio in my area, hoping to find relief and tranquility within its welcoming walls. As fate would have it, my journey from yoga to regular workouts at the studio led me to cross paths with a diverse array of individuals.

I do not believe in coincidences. If I believed, then I would certainly say that my life was littered with coincidences. Instead, I cling to the belief that every aspect of my story has been meticulously designed and orchestrated with purpose. It is through this lens that I recognize the profound hand of God guiding and shaping my life. There is a greater plan at work, one that transcends human comprehension.

One serendipitous encounter in 2011, before moving into my new home, changed the course of my life in unexpected ways. A prominent politician, aware of my previous teaching experience at my children's high school, approached me with an unusual request. He expressed a genuine concern for his thirteen-year-old son, whom I had taught during my brief tenure at the High school. He inquired if I could provide academic support by assisting his son with his homework after school.

Intrigued by the proposition, I carefully considered the offer and suggested that his wife contact me to discuss the logistics and fine-tune the details of this endeavor.

Shortly thereafter, the politician's wife reached out, expressing her gratitude for my willingness to assist their son. To my surprise, she also mentioned her nephew who could benefit greatly from the same academic guidance.

In an unexpected turn of events, I found myself beginning a journey of tutoring two young boys after school, nurturing their academic growth and igniting a passion within myself for education and mentorship.

What began as a small act of kindness and a genuine desire to support these eager minds soon gained momentum. Word began spreading and before I knew it, my humble efforts had birthed an unexpected business venture.

On reflection, these were truly remarkable circumstances. It was the hand of God once again guiding and propelling me to align my passion for teaching, my commitment to education and my love for children. My inadvertent foray into tutoring is a testament to the adage that success often finds us when we least expect it. It also shows that small acts of kindness can lead one on an extraordinary adventure.

My new business had begun without me even trying. This new vocation as an educator became an integral part of my life story, shaping my purpose and fulfilling my soul in ways I could not have foreseen.

When I moved into my new home, word began to spread and I began to focus on tutoring Biology and Chemistry. Over time, my intake of students saw me teaching seven days a week. My daughter also became a student of mine and went on to attain great success. She achieved first place in the Caribbean for her performance in Biology. She also went on to become the female Jamaica Scholar in 2017.

Fast forward to present day, my heart swells with perpetual wonder at the incredible accomplishments of my daughter. She embodies beauty, intelligence, and elegance and I could not be prouder of the remarkable young woman she has blossomed into. We were inseparable until my separation from her father, and I will forever hold close to my heart the memories of our cherished times together.

My son, also continues to amaze me. His success as an attorney fills me with immense pride. I vividly remember the days when we worked together, nurturing his reading abilities and fostering his comprehension skills. Now, my heart overflows with joy as I flip through the pages of the newspaper, discovering his well-deserved professional appointments. I am truly thrilled for him and the remarkable journey he is embarking upon.

Though I may find myself on the sidelines now, I remain a steadfast observer of both my children. I am filled with admiration as I witness the multitude of paths that lie before them. Even from a distance, I am in perpetual awe of their spirits, and I offer my blessings as I watch them navigate life's adventures.

I bless my children's journey.

CHAPTER 12

The Magazine

In 2015, another transformative event unfolded, forever leaving its imprint on my destiny. Destiny weaves an elaborate design, guiding the course of our lives, intertwining with our choices, shaping our journey and ultimate fulfilment. It is truly awe-inspiring to witness the exquisite orchestration of the universe as it conducts the twists and turns of life under the guidance of the divine maestro, the Almighty God.

It was during a momentous October day, when my phone rang, and a voice brimming with enthusiasm introduced herself as Janice, the owner of a local lifestyle magazine. Her bubbly personality radiated through the phone, as she made an unexpected proposition to feature me as the cover story for the December edition of her magazine. I found this strange, to say the least. Baffled, I questioned the reason behind the request, as I was no celebrity. Janice's explanation followed, revealing that she had heard about my beautiful home and was keen to showcase both its opulence and my own personal story in her publication. I was at a loss for words, I knew that this was a decision I had to make with my family before giving an answer.

Later that day, when my family had gathered in the family room, I shared the details of my conversation with Janice. Initially, my husband responded with a strong and immediate "no", expressing reservations about the feature. He explicitly did not want photos of his house to be featured. In contrast, both my children brimmed with excitement and they questioned their father's dissent. Sensing their genuine excitement, my husband eventually acquiesced, yielding to our children's eager desire to witness their mother's spotlight moment.

However, my husband's consent came with a set of conditions. He insisted on reviewing and approving all photographs of our home before granting permission for their publication.

And so, an unexpected friendship blossomed as I welcomed Janice into my home for my very first photo shoot. I was excited but anxious at the same time. It was scheduled for a Thursday afternoon when my daughter would be at school. She really wished to be present so we waited until she returned from school. In the meantime, my hair was styled and my make-up was done professionally. The wardrobe had been carefully selected some days before, clothing loaned from a prominent local store.

The photo shoot involved far more than I had expected, with multiple wardrobe and location changes. Throughout the process, Janice exhibited utmost professionalism and enthusiasm, making the experience enjoyable. As the photo shoot was coming to a close, my husband returned home, but his reception of Janice and her crew was lukewarm at best. Nonetheless, he had given consent to the feature.

Shortly after the photo shoot, Janice sent one of her best writers, Marsha, to interview me as well as to tour the home for the purpose of writing the feature story. During my interview with Marsha, she explained that she was also a publicist. She advised me that I should give my small tutoring business a registered name and that I should consider a marketing campaign. She volunteered to provide me with a proposal and estimate of marketing costs. The proposal would not come with a cost.

This intrigued me and I agreed. Shortly after, I received her comprehensive proposal and decided to hire her services. This marked a turning point in my career as everything began falling into place. I rebranded my business as "Bio and Chem Tutoring," admittedly not the most creative name, but it marked a significant milestone for me. In addition, television interviews and press releases were set in motion, leading to a rapid series of developments.

With the arrival of the December edition, the magazine was now out in the world, and as I stumbled upon copies displayed in pharmacies and supermarkets, a wave of self-consciousness washed over me. There it was – my own face staring back at me from the glossy covers, and the emotions that surged through me were a mix of thrill and surreal wonder.

During this same period, Marsha worked diligently, coordinating various marketing strategies to promote my tutoring business. As I ventured into the realm of television interviews, Marsha stepped in as my trusted coach, guiding me through the process.

The initial interview was undeniably nerve racking, with anxiety and self-doubt threatening to overshadow my words. These challenging experiences proved to be a powerful catalyst for personal growth. They pushed me beyond my comfort zone, instilling a fresh sense of confidence in me. They marked key moments of transformative growth, shaping me into a more assured and capable individual.

My children were thrilled by my newfound 'fame' and I tried to overcome my nervousness and face my new challenges and opportunities with optimism rather than anxiety. At the same time Marsha reached out to a national newspaper, proposing that I write a column in their Career and Education supplement appearing in their Sunday edition. Surprisingly, they agreed and so began my writing career.

Throughout this time of change and self-discovery, my husband's indifference remained constant, leaving me to question the sincerity of his support for my new endeavors. Despite the ambiguity, my children emerged as loyal cheerleaders, bursting with happiness and pride as they witnessed my articles being published in the newspaper. Their encouragement became a constant source of motivation and validation, reminding me that I was making strides in the right direction. To the best of my knowledge, my husband never read my articles.

Janice and I continued to keep in touch. We had not yet become good friends but we were sociable. My articles in the newspaper were well received and I was actually proud of myself, a rare occurrence.

As my writing journey continued, a new path emerged when I ventured into creating a workbook specifically tailored for High School Chemistry students, recognizing the existing demand. I approached a local publishing company and was pleasantly surprised as they welcomed the opportunity to publish my workbook. I also wrote articles for the same magazine in which I had been featured.

Once again, my children wholeheartedly accepted this new venture serving as an added motivation. In fact, I even proudly featured my daughter's image on the cover of this freshly minted workbook, a testament to our shared enthusiasm.

The authoring bug persisted within me, fueling my desire to offer guidance to parents seeking ways to enhance their children's academic performance. Drawing from my experience as a tutor and parent, I decided to pen a book dedicated to providing valuable insights and techniques. Parents frequently approached me on this topic, seeking advice, and I aimed to address their queries through my writing. Hence, was born *Yes! You Can Help Your Child Achieve Academic Success*, a self-published guide for parents.

Self-publishing was not nearly as easy as it appeared. However, with persistence and diligence, graphic artists and book formatters,

I was able to release the book in November 2016.

I *was now a published author*.

CHAPTER 13

The Allegations

*I*n 2016, another heart-wrenching occurrence transpired, shaking the very foundation of my world. As I reflect upon the journey I've traversed, it becomes evident that many of life's events are unpredictable and catch us completely off guard. No amount of preparation could have braced me for what occurred.

We are aware that death is an inevitable part of life. We understand that we may experience the loss of a loved one at some point. Yet, we never anticipate, nor can we fathom, the unexpected accusation of attempted rape against one's own husband. Such allegations strike with a force that leaves one stunned and utterly unprepared.

By 2016, my husband's professional endeavors had reached a pivotal point. While he still served as a director at the prominent company, he assumed full-time operations of his accountancy and audit firm, which conveniently operated from the comfort of our newly built home.

I had worked with the architect to design the home so that it had a separate office entrance and dedicated office, bathroom and kitchenette facilities for his staff. Among his employees, there was a young lady named Sandra who carried out the day-to-day operations under his supervision.

In an effort to provide convenience and ensure her safety, my husband frequently requested that either myself or one of our children pick her up from the nearby bus stop, sparing her the need to navigate the journey on foot.

They say wives possess a sixth sense, an intuitive perception that may very well be the voice of God speaking to us. In the case of Sandra, I always harbored an unsettling feeling deep within.

It was two days before my husband's birthday when he nonchalantly mentioned to me his intention to accompany Sandra to a client's office. She would need to be there for a couple days to tend to work-related matters.

On my husband's birthday, while our family was out for dinner, curiosity got the better of me. I inquired about Sandra and her progress at the client's office. With a seemingly casual demeanor, he assured me that everything was going well. Little did I know that beneath the surface, a series of peculiar events and a web of deceit was beginning to unravel.

In the days that followed, I observed an influx of unfamiliar faces clandestinely entering our home to meet with my husband behind closed doors. I felt uneasy.

The memory of that December morning in 2016 remains etched into my consciousness with striking clarity. In that moment, as my husband stepped into the kitchen where I stood, an inexplicable surge of intuition guided my words: "What's going on with all these people coming in and out? Are you about to be arrested?" It was as if an unseen force propelled those words from my lips.

His gaze met mine, and with a heavy sigh, he uttered the words that shattered the delicate fabric of my reality: "I have something to tell you, Sandra has accused me of attempted rape."

Time seemed to stand still as the weight of his confession enveloped me, suffocating the air around us. My heart pounded in my chest as the words echoed through the space between us – allegations of attempted rape. Even now I wonder, if this was but a dream.

The shockwave of disbelief reverberated through every fiber of my being, rendering me numb with incomprehension. It was a betrayal beyond comprehension, an unfathomable breach of trust that threatened to dismantle my world.

In that moment, the ground beneath me shifted, and I found myself grappling with an overwhelming sense of instability. My once solid foundation crumbled, leaving me adrift in a sea of uncertainty and doubt. How could this be happening? The realization pierced through the fog of denial as my husband confessed that he had known about the accusation even before his birthday, exposing a web of lies spun with callous disregard. In fact, at the time of his birthday, Sandra had already walked off the job. He had already sought legal counsel and had received emails from Sandra which he claimed to have been advised by his lawyer to delete. Therefore, I could not see these emails.

The whole situation was incomprehensible, unfathomable – an unthinkable betrayal. Lies and lies and more lies... what a web of lies! That's how it all seemed to me. In keeping with the laws of this country, he was to be arrested and then the prosecution would need to prove his guilt.

These allegations and possible arrest would obviously be a high-profile case in our country.

It would bring tremendous embarrassment, shame and public humiliation to our seemingly perfect family. It was unheard of and I was totally unprepared for such a turn in my life.

Of course, my husband vehemently denied the allegations. I do not know the truth. My instinct told me that this was a disgruntled ex-lover seeking retribution against my husband. Albeit, I also had to acknowledge that the allegations could possibly be true. Again, I do not claim to know the truth, but I do know that I was married to a deceptive man and a person I did not know.

What I do know was that the allegations were indeed made and that my husband expected that he would be arrested. We therefore faced the task of informing our children about the impending storm that would unleash a scandal of mega proportions. Their perfect world was about to be turned upside down.

In the days that followed, a suffocating atmosphere enveloped me. It felt as though every breath was a struggle. I attempted to push aside the persistent and relentless thoughts in my mind, which whispered that my husband had been unfaithful to me with that young lady. Deep within my being, I sensed that the allegations of attempted rape stemmed from a relationship that had turned sour, casting a shadow of doubt over the truth of the matter.

The weight of uncertainty pressed upon me, intensifying the emotional turmoil. As a mother, I wrestled with the responsibility of providing a safe haven for my children amidst the impending storm. I knew that I had to be their pillar of strength, even as my own foundation was trembling. The road ahead seemed treacherous, filled with unknown twists and turns that would challenge our resilience and test the bonds of our family.

In the face of this storm, my children clung fiercely to their firm belief that the allegations were nothing but fabrications and that Sandra was intentionally sowing seeds of discord. Their faith in their father remained unswerving, and they even entertained my husband's conspiracy theory that there were others conspiring with Sandra to orchestrate his downfall. Their loyalty to their father and their wish to safeguard him from harm clouded their judgment, stoking suspicions and creating complex narratives. My son, especially, was consumed by anger.

As a mother, it pained me to witness their blind loyalty which obscured their ability to perceive reality in its true light. While I understood their innate need to protect and support their father, I chose not to share my own suspicions with them. Deep down, I held onto the hope that they would eventually see through the elaborate web of falsehoods woven around us. In the depths of my heart, I wished for their eyes to open to the truth organically, without my intervention. I needed them to see beyond the façade and recognize the flaws and contradictions that existed within their father's narrative.

******

As I sat in stupor several days after the truth of the allegations emerged, I reflected on the years of my marriage and the troubling path it had taken. It was then that a suppressed memory began to resurface. I recalled an incident where my husband had engaged in a deceitful act of omission. It involved him purchasing a roundtrip airline ticket from Kingston to Canada for a woman he had business dealings with, using our shared credit card points.

He had failed to realize that the credit card company would send me an email confirmation, as the email address they had on record was mine. This clandestine purchase raised significant suspicions, and upon confronting him, he explained that the woman had experienced a death in her family and needed to attend a funeral in Canada, requesting his assistance for the ticket. He claimed that he did not believe it was necessary to inform me of this purchase. Perhaps, I may appear unsympathetic, but I could not help but question the covert nature of this action, which inevitably left me pondering the true nature of his relationship with this woman, yet another instance where my intuition screamed at me to listen and take heed. Still, I did nothing. I kept quiet and remained the dutiful wife.

As I continued to contemplate our circumstances, another episode crossed my mind – an occurrence both perplexing and thought-provoking. While our present abode was taking shape, my husband ventured into obtaining two additional real estate holdings. Strikingly, even though I voiced my concerns, my name remained noticeably absent from the titles of these properties. This omission left me with questions and an unsettling sense of inadequacy leading me to wrestle with feelings of unworthiness and insignificance.

After decades of marriage, it was disheartening to realize that my husband seemed resolute in safeguarding his own interests. It was as if he had an innate foresight that our marital bonds would not endure the tests of time. Perhaps he reached this conclusion based on his own actions and decisions, but I remain uncertain of his motivations. All I can attest to, is the deliberate sidelining I experienced, making me feel like a mere bystander rather than a cherished partner and wife.

As my contemplation drew to a close, I confronted the sobering reality that no amount of wishful thinking could alter my circumstances. The hope of a fulfilling marriage had become futile. It was evident that our union was destined for failure, and my husband had seemingly prepared himself for this inevitability.

*****

Delving into the complexities of the days and weeks that followed the revelation of the allegations is a task I cannot easily undertake. Suffice it to say, arrangements were made to secure my husband's bail, should the need arise, a task made challenging by my limited knowledge of his financial affairs and my restricted access to his funds.

Sometime later, Sandra withdrew her statement and no charges were brought against my husband, but the injury and devastation wreaked on our marriage was already done and was irreparable.

The weight of that allegation was heavy and I could no longer wear the blindfold of ignorance. I had to open my eyes and face reality. There was never going to be a 'happily ever after'. The wounds inflicted upon our marriage ran too deep, leaving us unable to find solace or restoration.

The truth had clawed its way to the surface demanding to be seen and heard. I did not know what to do. Fear, societal norms and expectations abounded in my heart. I just did not know what to do. I needed to confront the bitter and painful truth and find the strength to rewrite my story. "All was not lost," I thought, "my children's love would always be there". If only I had known that the monster would also take that away from me.

The monster takes all.

CHAPTER 14

First, Do No Harm

*E*arlier that same year, around July 2016, I found myself facing another medical challenge. This time it concerned my eyes. I sought the expertise of various specialists in the field to determine the best course of action. I decided on a doctor whose child I was tutoring at the time.

I trusted this doctor. He was kind, empathetic and was willing and able to help. His professionalism and apparent competence in his specialized field reinforced my belief in his abilities. At that time, he was in his early fifties, married and I was in my late forties, a married female seeking professional assistance.

The diagnosis revealed another autoimmune disease, uveitis. It seemed as if my subconscious self was relentlessly seeking an end to my troubled life. Struggling with self-acceptance and self-love, my body was seeking avenues for its own demise. However, even in the depths of despair, I have come to realize that God never abandons us and always has a greater plan in store.

The nature of my illness necessitated frequent visits to the doctor's office. The recurrent nature of my condition demanded close monitoring and careful management. It was through these repeated encounters, coupled with the fact that I was also tutoring his daughter, that a certain level of friendship and familiarity began to develop between us.

Shortly after Christmas, right after the nightmare involving the allegations 'went away', an unfortunate incident occurred involving my son. It was at a party where we suspect he may have been intentionally drugged. He spent hours in hospital receiving intravenous fluids. It appeared to be a sinister act targeting affluent youngsters, possibly for kidnapping and ransom demands.

Close to the new year, on another routine visit to the doctor, I shared this personal experience. I recounted what had happened to my son, not only as a cautionary tale but also to ensure the safety of his own daughter. Understandably, he was alarmed, displaying the concern any parent would in such circumstances.

He offered to pray with me. It is worth noting that he was a seemingly devout Christian actively involved in his church. He held my hands and he prayed for the well-being of myself and my family.

The year 2017 dawned upon us, and we clung to the hope that it would bring about better days. My treatment for uveitis appeared to be yielding positive results, and I was satisfied with my progress. My communication with the doctor primarily revolved around professional matters through WhatsApp. If my eyes showed signs of redness, a characteristic symptom, I would reach out to him, and he would promptly prescribe necessary medications.

Then, around February, something unexpected occurred. My doctor sent me a friend request on Facebook. I found it slightly unusual but I decided to accept the invitation nonetheless. To my surprise, as soon as I accepted, as if he was waiting, he initiated a call through Facebook. This also struck me as unusual. I did not answer the call. He then texted "Thank you for accepting my invite".

Shortly after that incident, the doctor sent me an unexpected message on WhatsApp early one morning. He invited me to accompany him to a conference happening on that same day. It immediately raised a red flag in my mind. I shared the text with my husband, hoping for some emotional reaction from him, but he remained impassive and simply advised me to decline the invitation.

Although I felt flattered by the invitation, I realized the inappropriateness of the situation. I mustered the courage to call him and express my reservations. He assured me that his intentions were innocent, but then he went on to request that I call him by his first name. This marked a shift in our relationship.

Even though I did not attend the conference with him, a peculiar sort of friendship started to develop. He messaged me afterwards, sharing details about the conference, leaving me confused.

At the time, I did not realize that I was being sexually groomed for an affair. With therapy and my own research, I now have a better understanding of the events that transpired.

My grooming was incremental. It was not an overnight occurrence. The doctor displayed patience, while his actions were calculated to ensnare me. Looking back, I wonder how I could ever have let it go so far. I am a well-educated and successful female, so how did this happen? How could I have allowed this?

The answer lies in the strategies and tactics that were used to ensnare me and in my own naivety and emotional vulnerability.

Let me be clear, I do not exclusively blame the

doctor for what occurred. I take responsibility for my own actions and choices. At the time, I was struggling with low self-esteem and was desperately hungry for attention and affection which were sorely lacking in my marriage.

Looking back, my office visits were more or less normal, though I did notice a little extra attention, a smile, a light touch when none was required. Thinking the best of him, I assumed any light touch was just him being friendly. Now I know this was just part of the process of sexual grooming.

The first touch prepared him for the second and then the third touch. Eventually, he began to hug me as I would leave his office. A very slight hug as if to say "Don't worry, all will be well soon". It seemed innocent enough, but what he was actually doing was trapping me by forging an attachment bond. I became attached to the doctor that was caring for me.

Over time, the emotional bond intensified as the doctor continued to correspond through WhatsApp. He assumed the role of counsellor in my life. He was helpful, accessible and gave good advice. Our conversations via WhatsApp were filled with unfamiliar emojis, particularly an abundance of hugging emojis. I now understand that he was cultivating the attachment bond between us.

I have learnt that sexual grooming is a process

in which a perpetrator gradually establishes emotional bonds and trust with their intended victim, often by exploiting vulnerabilities and manipulating their emotions. Through seemingly innocent actions, such as providing attention, support, and affection, the groomer creates an illusion of care and compassion. They employ subtle techniques to undermine boundaries, gradually normalizing inappropriate behaviors and blurring the lines between friendship and intimacy. Victims are usually individuals experiencing dissatisfaction or emotional neglect within their existing relationship, making them more susceptible to seeking emotional connection elsewhere.

Unfortunately, this was the case with me, as my relationship with my husband became even more strained after the episode with the allegations. In my estimation, by that juncture, my marriage had effectively breathed its last breath.

I was not entirely oblivious to the boundaries that were perilously being crossed between myself and the doctor. I realized that I had become emotionally attached to the doctor and that I was unwittingly in the midst of an emotional affair.

I even mustered the courage to confront him about the inappropriate undertones threading through our friendship. I expressed my concerns, pointing out the potential harm and the blurred lines we were treading. The doctor skillfully dismissed my worries, assuring me that there was nothing wrong with our friendship.

He possessed a knack for diverting the conversation, swiftly changing topics to avoid addressing the underlying issues. Despite these red flags, I found myself unable to resist the intoxicating allure of his attention and approval.

I vividly recall one conversation where I inquired if his wife was aware of our frequent communication. He admitted that she had no knowledge of our interactions. Similarly, my husband was cognizant of our friendship but remained unaware of the extent of our connection.

In spite of all my misgivings, I found myself unable to break free from the grip of this emotional entanglement. It was as if I had become ensnared in a mesh of dependency, craving the validation and affirmation he so readily provided. My already fragile self-esteem left me vulnerable, making me an easy target for the allure of an emotional affair.

It is essential to acknowledge the complexity of emotional affairs and the multitude of emotions they entail. The mixture of guilt, desire, and self-deception created a turbulent whirlwind within me. I was torn between the awareness of the wrongness of our actions and the overpowering emotions that kept me entangled in this forbidden relationship.

It is unfortunate that my lack of self-esteem made me extraordinarily susceptible to this doctor's manipulations. The absence of a solid foundation of self-worth made me prone to seeking affirmation and affection outside the confines of my committed relationship.

In this web of emotions, the emotional affair took root, fueled by the intoxicating mix of attention, approval, and vulnerability. It became a dangerous dance, one that I had unwittingly entered but struggled to escape. This inappropriate dynamic continued for months but nothing overtly inappropriate had happened. Many times, I thought "we are just friends, that hug was just a friendly hug," as if to reassure myself.

Then it happened, in his office, an incident that shattered the illusion of safety within his office, a supposed professional space. The professional visit was over and he asked for a hug as I was leaving. This hug felt distinctly different. His grip tightened, his hands caressed my upper and lower back, leaving me frozen and unable to react. All the while, he whispered, "relax, relax, relax," his actions continuing as he playfully tousled my hair, maintaining physical contact for what felt like an eternity. The weight of shame held me captive. I froze, but eventually, I managed to pull away.

Then, as if nothing happened, he instructed me to fix my disheveled hair and I complied silently. I said nothing. I walked out of his office, making my next appointment.   He instructed the receptionist not to charge me, a futile attempt to obscure the gravity of what occurred.

I sought refuge in the rest room overwhelmed by emotions. I vomited and cried feeling violated, molested and very ashamed. The weight of shame can be a powerful force that compels both young and old victims of abuse to remain silent about their traumatic experiences.

Shame has the ability to silence victims, as it forces them to grapple with feelings of guilt, embarrassment, and self-blame. The fear of judgment and disbelief from others, as well as the worry that they may be blamed for the abuse, can further contribute to this silence. It was this same shame that caused me to remain silent when the Physics teacher molested me.

In this situation, I was consumed by a paralyzing fear that my husband would shift all the blame onto me. The thought of shouldering the weight of his accusations and facing his anger and the potential consequences was incredibly daunting and overwhelming.

A few days later, I called the doctor to address the issue of his inappropriate actions. I was intent on expressing my disapproval and drawing a clear boundary. He was standoffish and his response was that he had done nothing wrong. He denied everything, to a point where I even doubted my own memory and sanity. It was a classic case of gaslighting, where he manipulated my perception and made me question my own sanity.

He dismissed his actions as harmless, claiming that I simply appeared in need of a hug and he provided one. He denied that he had crossed a line. In the face of his denials, a seed of doubt took root within me, causing me to question the very fabric of my own recollections. Doubts began to creep in, as I wondered if I had somehow fabricated or misinterpreted the situation, and if my longing for validation had clouded my judgment. Was I to blame after all?

Once again, I was experiencing gaslighting, similar to what my husband had done years before. This tool used by narcissists aims to control and dominate others by distorting their reality and undermining their sense of self.

One might assume that I would have promptly cut ties, discontinuing my visits to him as my doctor and ending our friendship. In hindsight, that would have been the correct course of action. But, like a moth drawn to a mesmerizing flame, I inexplicably persisted, resolute in pursuing a path that held the potential to utterly devastate my life.

Reflecting upon the circumstances that led me to maintain contact with him, I find myself grappling with a perplexing question: why did I continue to engage in correspondence despite the complexities of our relationship? Was my addiction so strong that I could not disengage?

This entanglement took a toll not only on my emotional well-being but also had physical repercussions, leading to an unexpected battle with hypertension despite having always had a steady low blood pressure. I personally believe that the appearance of this new affliction was a result of the conflict within my mind, body and soul.

Even with all that had taken place, I continued my friendship with the doctor and he became my sole source of emotional support. In return, he peeled back the layers of his own life, exposing vulnerabilities that drew us closer together. Our lives became intertwined forming a deep emotional connection.

With each passing day, my addiction to the attention and approval he offered grew stronger. I became increasingly dependent on our connection, seeking solace in the emotional intimacy we shared. The voids in my life and my lack of self-worth amplified my vulnerability, further fueling the flames of this emotional affair. I longed for his presence, his words of affirmation, and the fleeting moments of happiness that came from our interactions.

Recognizing that I was on a slippery slope, I enlisted the help of two psychologists. I was desperate to help to navigate the turmoil within me. Suicidal ideation began to grip me once again, convincing me that escape through death was the only way out of this suffocating situation. Unfortunately, instead of finding resolution, the situation spiraled further out of control, intensifying the complexities which I was already grappling with.

In 2018, everything changed when he kissed me. I kissed him back, and in that moment, the line between friendship and something more was blurred. Though it never escalated to a sexual relationship, the repercussions of that moment were far-reaching. The damage had been inflicted, leaving me questioning the choices I had made. Yet, even as a new physical line had been crossed, the doctor elected to overlook the incident. We continued in our friendship pretending that nothing untoward had occurred.

Looking back, I feel an overwhelming sense of shame regarding my compliance and vulnerability in relation to that man. The person I was then stands in stark contrast to who I have become today. I acknowledge my weakness during that period. Even so, the devastation resulting from my frailty and misguided choices has ultimately fueled my growth and transformed me into a stronger individual.

As I contemplate the details of this messy affair, I am compelled to face the responsibility that lies within me for allowing the seeds of an emotional affair to take root and thrive. I take ownership of my own actions in succumbing to the allure of his attention and approval. It is crucial that I acknowledge the choices I made and the role I played in blurring the boundaries, as difficult as it may be. By accepting responsibility, I am able to confront my own weaknesses and strive towards personal growth and healing.

At the same time, I also feel empathy for the doctor, knowing that he must have also been going through a difficult time emotionally. He also had broken his marital vows, and that would have been a huge burden to carry. I can imagine that he was feeling a lot of guilt and shame, and that he may have been struggling with his own sense of self-worth.

Looking ahead, I am resolute in my quest to rediscover my worth and to heal. I am determined to break free from the chains of past trauma and seek a future that radiates with strength and empowerment.

I aspire to find a partner skilled in effective communication, one who grasps the significance of honest conversation and attentive listening. Most importantly, I deserve a love that places my well-being at its core, where I'm treasured, esteemed, and made a priority throughout our shared journey. In nurturing this vision, my aim is to cultivate a harmonious partnership grounded in mutual respect, understanding and support.

I am a work in progress.

CHAPTER 15

Consequences

In August of the same year, 2018, both my children started sensing something amiss in my relationship with the doctor. They shared their concerns with their dad, who then invited me to have a drink at a quiet establishment. The unusualness of the request filled me with alarm, and I suspected it had something to do with the doctor. I was filled with fear and trepidation in anticipation of what was soon to occur.

My intuition proved to be correct, and during the meeting, my husband confronted me about the situation. I mustered the courage to confess, revealing the nature of my emotional affair with the doctor. That moment catalyzed the rapid unraveling of my marriage, leading down a path of inevitable dissolution. As I watched my husband storm off in anger,

I dreaded the consequences to my hurtful confession. I understood that there would be no absolution, and the price I would have to pay for my missteps would be dire.

The weight of my mistakes burdened me, but I held onto the belief that my children's love for me was unshakable, just as my love for them. I knew the seriousness of the fracture my actions had caused, and it was essential that they hear the truth from me.

And so, sitting around the breakfast table, I summoned the courage to bare the truth of my inappropriate friendship with the doctor. Tears streamed down my face as I admitted to my mistakes. Overwhelmed by emotions, I abruptly rose from my seat and rushed upstairs, seeking refuge in the confines of my bathroom.

My son, driven by love, chased after me, wrapping his arms around me in a comforting embrace. After I composed myself, I found a loving note from my daughter beside my bed. It said, "no matter what, we love you." I felt an overwhelming surge of emotions. It was an act of love and forgiveness that touched my core, an act that still brings tears to my eyes as I struggle to reconcile it with subsequent turn of events.

The contrast between my daughter's note of love, and the compassion shown by my son, followed by their later estrangement, is a contradiction that leaves me grappling with confusion. The possibility that I may have irreparably damaged that sacred bond between mother and child is sometimes too much to handle. I did not expect it, I could not conceive it.

With my confession and admission of guilt came the inevitable penalties. I use the term "inevitable" because such was the nature of the person I was married to. Our relationship often took on a dictatorial tone, leaving me feeling like a child with him playing the role of a father figure.

The imbalance of power meant that my voice held little weight in many aspects of our life together. Now, faced with my wrongdoings, I had to endure humiliation and shame, as if deserving punishment for my perceived 'evil' ways. A part of me even internalized this belief, convinced that I deserved such treatment as penance for my actions.

My husband moved out of the master bedroom and relocated into the guest bedroom. He removed my credit cards leaving me with only one that at the time, was the only credit card I had that would send him a notification as soon as it was used. I was restricted to using it solely at the supermarket and pharmacy. He would even sometimes cross check the bills with the groceries bought.

My husband forbade me from receiving any visitors including my brothers or mother, and I, like a child obeyed. I vividly recall a particular incident involving my brother John. He was forced to park a few meters from my gate, while I hurriedly stepped out to collect a document he had brought for me. It was a heart-wrenching realization that I was trapped within a gilded cage. Yet, I complied, a testament to my shattered spirit.

In an attempt to seek justice, my son and husband sought legal counsel, contemplating arresting the doctor on charges of attempted rape. They firmly believed that the doctor had crossed an ethical and professional line and they felt that legal action was justified.

The gravity of the situation overwhelmed me, leaving me at a loss for how to process the unfolding events. I felt vulnerable. I felt like a child as I was led into the office of a prominent lawyer by my own son, completely submitting to the whims of my children and my husband.

During this turmoil, I grappled with conflicting emotions. While I understood the genuine concern and protective instincts of my loved ones, I could not bring myself to accuse the doctor of attempted rape. Deep down, I did not believe that the label of attempted rape was truly fitting.

In an act of transparency, I found the courage to share the situation with the doctor, disclosing the intent of my husband and children to pursue legal action against him. I chose to be honest. It was a difficult decision, as it meant diverging from the path my family had chosen, but I firmly believed in the importance of integrity and the pursuit of truth.

My husband discovered my communication with the doctor via WhatsApp and Facebook. It appeared that he had somehow obtained my phone records, possibly through means that were less than honest.

This discovery of my conversation further exacerbated the already tense atmosphere, fueling the anger and sense of betrayal felt by my children and husband. My husband's verbal abuse escalated, with his words cutting deep into my already wounded spirit.

At this juncture, it is important to highlight that the doctor, who played a role in the breakdown of my marriage, abruptly severed all communication with me. Despite being a supposed 'friend,' he showed no concern for my well-being, even though he knew that my husband, now aware of the emotional affair, was determined to unleash his wrath upon me. This only compounded the distress and deepened the sense of isolation I experienced during that trying period.

In the face of my compassionate disclosure regarding my family's intention to take legal action, the doctor chose to prioritize self-preservation, leaving me grappling with conflicting emotions regarding his decisions. Perhaps, he had valid reasons to safeguard his interests, though I wrestled with understanding this fully. Furthermore, he took the step of having his lawyer send me a letter, formally announcing his decision to discontinue as my doctor and instructing me to collect my patient file from his legal representative's office. I felt used and discarded.

The very same doctor resorted to fabricating tales in an attempt to create a false front, asserting that my belief that we had engaged in an emotional affair were mere figments of my imagination, bearing no truth whatsoever. He insinuated that I might be mentally unstable and had simply concocted the entire affair as a mere daydream.

As a result, I found myself sinking in a sea of darkness, overwhelmed by feelings of betrayal, despair and self-condemnation. I could not comprehend that someone who claimed to care and to be my friend could be so callous. I became consumed in a suffocating sense of being the worst person to walk this earth.

Subsequently, upon the conclusion that pursuing action through the courts would prove arduous, it was decided by my husband and children that I should report the doctor to the medical council as his actions flagrantly violated ethical boundaries by engaging in a romantic relationship with a patient.

In compliance with the wishes of my family, I filed the report, hoping it would somehow alleviate the pain and wrongs they felt had been inflicted on them. When I eventually left the marriage, I chose to discontinue those proceedings. I did not want to pursue any legal or disciplinary action, as I recognized my own role in the messy incident. All I desired was total closure.

This episode with the doctor served as the final blow to an already crumbling marriage. While I bear full responsibility for my misguided actions in this instance, it is important to recognize that the marriage itself was flawed from the beginning, with both parties failing to invest genuine effort into repairing its cracks.

This experience further underscores the significance of being cautious when placing blind faith in individuals who claim to be friends. In my perspective, the doctor's intention in befriending me was solely driven by the pursuit of a sexual encounter and not a true friendship. This only deepened my already existing sense of low self-esteem, as I, at that point in my marriage, had come to believe that my sole worth to my husband lay in being a caregiver to our children and a partner in the bedroom.

I faced the harsh consequences of my misdeeds not only externally, but internally as well, as the effects of my actions permeated the very essence of my being, stirring a raging storm of self-condemnation and an ardent yearning for redemption.

Within the confines of my own home, I felt trapped, stripped of my freedom and autonomy. I was weak and I did not fight for myself, my dignity and my self-respect. I allowed my husband to trample upon me and in turn, my children learned to disregard and disrespect me. Even while I remained in the same home, a stifling silence enveloped our interactions, with my children barely uttering a word to me.

The devious nature of my husband's emotional and financial abuse, coupled with the oppressive rules he imposed on me, left me psychologically battered and drained. On many occasions I once again considered suicide as a way to free myself from the all-consuming pain that had become my life.

The constant onslaught of belittlement and verbal abuse that ensued in the days and weeks after my confession, chipped away at my already diminished sense of self, leaving me a shadow of the person I once was. I became a prisoner within the walls of my own home, held captive by fear, doubt and the control exerted by my husband. My husband had appointed himself judge, jury and executioner and I had been judged and condemned.

I bear the weight of regret for not asserting myself and standing up against the mistreatment I endured. I enabled my children to be disrespectful to me. I did not affirm my undeniable status as their mother. This had a profound impact on my mental health and the dynamics within my family.

During this time, my husband initially agreed to join me in seeking marriage counseling from a Christian therapist. Once again, his behavior exhibited typical narcissistic traits. During just one session, he succumbed to anger, shouting relentlessly at me while hurling accusations, and then he walked out of the session. Our counseling together came to an abrupt halt from that point onward, never to be resumed.

This incident highlighted his lack of genuine interest in mending our relationship. I continued attending counseling sessions on my own with the same therapist driven by a desire to unearth the imperfections within my own psyche. At the same time, we also had friends willing to offer free counseling, even making the offer to come to our home, yet my husband adamantly declined their support.

Thus, it became distinct that there was no way to salvage our fractured relationship. The responsibility for healing could not rest solely on my shoulders; a marriage involves two individuals who must share an equal commitment to its restoration. This principle applies universally to any relationship, emphasizing the crucial role of dedication and prioritization in nurturing and sustaining meaningful connections.

In light of these circumstances, the cycle of emotional and financial abuse persisted relentlessly, showing no signs of abating. I found myself entirely dependent on my husband's whims, trapped within his sphere of control.

As my tutoring business generated only modest income, it became my sole means of supporting my personal expenses. I grew uncomfortable carrying cash around. Consequently, I approached a bank to acquire my own personal credit card. Given my status as a self-employed individual with minimal resources and lacking the assistance of an accountant (a role my husband had always fulfilled), I had no choice but to provide cash as collateral for this credit card. It was an embarrassing and belittling experience, yet I ultimately obtained my own credit card, marking a significant step towards reclaiming some measure of financial independence.

Notably, even with my husband's relocation from the master bedroom, he continued to expect sexual favors, seemingly unaffected by the emotional turmoil and detachment that had enveloped our relationship.

As his fiftieth birthday approached in November of that same year, he decided to throw himself a party. The stark reality of our splintered union became painfully apparent as he cryptically informed me that he would at a later time let me know if I was invited.

I was always the event planner in the family, but I always included my children, so they knew what to do. They planned the event without my help. Nonetheless, as the big day drew closer, I noticed glaring omissions in the necessary supplies. I approached my husband, reminding him of the items that had not been procured. I offered assistance to acquire them at a specific store in Kingston. He accepted my offer.

It so happened that this store only accepted a particular credit card which was one that my husband had removed from my possession, so he handed it back to me for the purpose of completing the shopping expedition. I completed my mission. As soon as I stepped into the home, my husband demanded the immediate return of the credit card, in a most ungracious manner, disregarding my kindness in obtaining the necessary supplies.

The day of the party came, and the stage was set. Some dishes were prepared at our home and some dishes were being catered. As the guests began to trickle in, an undeniable sense of exclusion permeated the air.

One could not help but notice the absence of my relatives and friends from the guest list, a stark contrast to the predominantly unfamiliar faces that flooded our home. The few guests that I knew all inquired about the strange absence of my mom and brothers who were always present at my parties and functions. Unsure of the appropriate response, I redirected their queries to my husband, a strategy that only deepened the mystery of their absence.

The attendees were primarily my husband's clients, giving the event the air of a corporate event rather than a personal celebration. One could even believe it was an office party. The ambiance felt oddly detached from the warmth and familiarity I had come to expect at our gatherings.

My husband sought to create an illusion of happiness and harmony in our strained marriage. We were photographed with his arm draped around me, a smokescreen of matrimonial bliss. He introduced me to his clients, individuals I had never met before, as if we were a picture-perfect couple. In that moment, we played our roles convincingly, expertly concealing the fractures and deep-rooted discontent that lay beneath the surface. Myself and our children gathered around him during the cake-cutting ceremony, pretending that everything was absolutely normal.

On reflection, it became apparent that the party served as more than just a festive occasion. It was a charade meticulously orchestrated by my husband, aimed at projecting an image of unity and contentment to the outside world. The discrepancies between the public façade and the private reality were haunting and my heart screamed in distress. One well-known trait of a narcissist is their ability to appear amiable, polite, and helpful to individuals outside their inner circle. This characteristic often leads people to doubt the victim's claims, as the narcissist's charming disguise makes it challenging for others to believe the truth. Such was the case with my husband.

The celebration of my husband's fiftieth birthday served as a partial catalyst, bringing my children back to me, albeit in a somewhat half-hearted manner. My children and I were once again engaging in our usual conversations filled with laughter and love. Still, there was a strain on our relationship.

At this point I should mention that immediately following the confession of my emotional affair, my husband imposed a strange and absurd rule that my children were not allowed to ride in my vehicle, citing the presence of the doctor who had occasionally sat in it. This directive made no logical sense but my assessment of the situation and my knowledge of the superstitious nature of my husband, is that he felt that the spirit of the doctor was still in my car. I know that sounds absolutely ridiculous, and it is, but that was the twisted nature of the monster I was married to. It also showcased how he controlled my children into disrespecting me.

My adult children did abide by the directive, but in December of that year my daughter decided that it made no sense and she resumed travelling with me occasionally.

The consequences were harsh.

CHAPTER 16

The Launch

$\mathcal{P}$rior to all that upheaval, in the same year of 2018, I was appointed Chairman of the Friends of the Bustamante Hospital for Children (FBHC), the hospital that had saved my life when I was only six months old. This was my entry into philanthropy.

This appointment occurred a few months before the marital separation but even then, it did not meet with my husband's approval. I hypothesized that this was due to his continued insecurities about my becoming a public figure. He also said that my time would be better spent doing something for which I was being paid.

This new role came with a number of duties and I found myself having to speak at certain events. I also had to attend meetings with many prominent individuals and I was learning the art of fundraising. I was slowly metamorphosizing into a more confident person.

As part of our fundraising efforts, a major event was planned for February 2019. It was decided that a launch of this event would be prudent and that my home would be an excellent location for this occasion. Of course, I would require my husband's permission in order to agree to host the event. Intuitively, I knew my husband would approve this event, as it presented an opportunity for him to interact with influential individuals and potentially promote his business.

I had the discussion with my husband and he approved on condition that he vetted the guest list. With his approval secured, myself and the team began planning a fabulous event for the first week of January 2019. We actively sought sponsors, sent out invitations, finalized food and drink arrangements and coordinated décor. Despite the excitement, I couldn't help but feel disappointed as once again, none of my family or friends could be included on the guest list as per my husband's orders.

Meanwhile, my dissatisfaction with my living conditions began to gnaw at my spirit, intensifying the already unbearable discord within the household. The weight of this distress pushed me to the brink, leading me down a treacherous state of mind where suicidal thoughts increased in frequency.

My deep-rooted aversion to conflict and confrontation made it difficult for me to confront and address my personal problems head-on. Instead, I typically resort to burying them deep within, hoping they would vanish on their own. This coping mechanism, though temporarily shielding me from turmoil, only fueled a cycle of unhappiness and unresolved issues. With each passing day, the discontentment grew, festering like an open wound. I found myself teetering on the edge of a precipice, swaying between mental stability and instability.

As the big day of the launch approached, I had reason to visit a popular jewelry store. It was there that I had the pleasure of encountering the charismatic Mark, a distinguished executive from a well-known finance company. The timing could not have been more fortuitous, as I, in my role as Chairman of the FBHC, had been actively pursuing a partnership with a financial institution.

I received his telephone number and made contact the next day. He was responsive and immediately had his team reach out to me to make arrangements to assist the FBHC. With the launch just one week away I extended an invitation to Mark.

Within a few days of making contact with Mark, and before the launch, Mark began flirting with me by text. I was surprised and flattered. I consequently agreed to meet him at his home the morning after the launch. As I reflect on this decision, it makes no logical sense. It was completely out of character for me.

What occurred next puts me in a very unfavourable light. My actions during those first three weeks of 2019 cannot be explained or justified. I hated my life; I lacked direction and undoubtedly, I was spiraling towards self-destruction. It was an intentional move to inflict self-harm.

Mark was astute and exuded power. He possessed qualities that appealed to me – sweetness, kindness, and intelligence – leading me down a road where without a doubt, I must have known what to expect. As the saying goes, "one thing led to another," and we found ourselves in an intimate encounter. This was the first time I had been intimate with a man other than my husband.

My decision to engage in such an act during our very first significant meeting remains perplexing. It was an uncharacteristic act of rebellion. Perhaps, in some twisted way, I was intentionally sabotaging my own marriage, almost as if I were seeking to declare my freedom. Although I was separated from my husband, we had still maintained physical relations. My husband, aware that I had not been intimate with the doctor, was still open to intimacy.

Deep inside, I understood that once I crossed the boundary of intimacy with someone else, our marriage would be irreparably damaged, as my husband would consider me 'tainted' and 'dirty'.

Engaging in intimacy with Mark was not driven by a desire for a meaningful relationship but rather fueled by a vindictive impulse to inflict deep pain upon my husband. It strangely felt liberating, almost as if it symbolized an act of reclaiming my power. Although I longed for true affection from a partner, I did not anticipate discovering it in Mark. I was pleasantly surprised.

Nevertheless, in my pursuit of revenge, I inflicted intense damage upon myself and, unwittingly and unintentionally, upon my children. The effects of my actions would reverberate far beyond the boundaries of a crumbling marriage, leaving scars that may never heal.

Revenge is a destructive cycle that offers fleeting satisfaction but long-lasting consequences.

CHAPTER 17

The Fairy Tale Ends

In the depths of my mind, I had convinced myself that the encounter with Mark would be nothing more than a fleeting 'one-night stand.' I did not anticipate the surprising depth of Mark's character and his commitment to continued communication. His genuine affection and care began to shine through, defying my initial expectations.

It was a mere two days after that intimate encounter that a moment of self-sabotage unfolded. Unconsciously, I left my laptop open, perhaps subconsciously seeking to expose my actions. My husband, driven by disregard for my privacy, discovered my conversation with Mark on WhatsApp. In that moment, the truth of my encounter was unveiled, and my husband became aware of the intimate connection.

It was around 7:00 pm when he stormed into my bedroom, his rage palpable as he ordered me to pack a bag and leave his house immediately. The air in the room grew heavy with tension as my husband's anger consumed the space. Fear coursed through my veins, knowing the depth of his wrath. It is significant to note that my husband referred to our shared home as solely 'his' house, further highlighting the imbalance of power within our relationship.

The weight of my actions pressed upon me, as the results of my choices unfolded before my eyes. While he never resorted to physical violence, the intensity of his gestures, tone of voice, and facial expressions made it abundantly clear that the threat of physical violence was very much real.

My mind spun in a whirlwind, attempting to grasp the immense gravity of the situation. I found myself in uncharted territory, facing circumstances I had never encountered before. I was at a loss as to how to respond or what steps to take next. The overwhelming uncertainty left me feeling disoriented and I was unsure where to seek refuge.

It was a jarring realization that despite this being our shared home, I was being chased out as though I were an insignificant creature. Fear gripped me tightly, constricting my every thought and movement. Tears streaming down my face, I began packing a bag under the watchful gaze of my husband. It seemed he was suspicious, as though I might 'steal' something, even though I was in my own home. Yes, it was my own home, but I felt like an unwelcome guest. With a heavy heart, I made my way to my car, unsure of what the future held.

In the midst of the chaos, as I hurriedly reversed my car, my panic, stress, and sheer disarray caused an accidental collision with one of my husband's cars, serving as a physical manifestation of the intense emotions that consumed me in that moment.

As I drove out, tears streaming down my face, I called Mark, a man I had known only a couple of days. As I poured out the events that had occurred, I detected a hint of surprise in his voice. He was still at his office, but his kindness and concern resonated through the phone as he instructed me to make my way to his house, assuring me that he would join me shortly.

As I continued driving, the ringing of my phone shattered the silence of the car. It was my husband, his voice commanding and demanding. Confusion clouded my mind, leaving me susceptible to his orders. In my bewildered state, I succumbed to his demand of me returning home. I turned my car around, retracing the road back to the very place I was just unceremoniously driven out. I am not sure why I was instructed to return home. Perhaps my husband himself was confused and hurt and felt a semblance of guilt.

The events that occurred immediately after are a blur in my memory. I was in a dazed and uncertain state, unsure of what steps to take next. I had chosen to engage in an intimate relationship with Mark, fully aware that there would be repercussions. I acknowledge that this was not the appropriate or honorable way to bring closure to my marriage.

I also recognize the gravity of my actions and the impact they had on myself, my husband, and my children. I can only begin to imagine the sheer shock and disbelief that must have consumed my husband upon discovering my indiscretion with someone I barely knew. It is striking to consider the fact that despite having known the doctor for an extended period of time, I had firmly upheld boundaries. Yet, I had allowed myself to cross those boundaries with Mark, traversing uncharted territory with reckless abandon.

The details of what was communicated to my children regarding this latest transgression remain unclear to me. We never had that conversation, as their expressions made it evident, they were already informed. Their disappointment was palpable, and an intense sense of shame washed over me. I acknowledge that I acted timidly by not addressing the matter with them promptly. In retrospect, my failure to openly communicate only compounded the weight of the situation.

It is clear to me now that I should have pursued a more respectful and considerate way to end my marriage, one that prioritized open communication, empathy, and mutual understanding. I deeply regret the pain caused by my choices.

The certainty of divorce brought with it a complex array of emotions. I was filled with conflicting feelings. On one hand, there was a sense of relief, a recognition that my marriage had reached an impasse and needed to come to an end. On the other hand, dread and uncertainty gripped my heart as I faced the prospect of navigating life as a single individual. The magnitude of this life-altering decision weighed heavily upon me, particularly considering my lack of a stable job and the fact that I had never experienced the solitude of being alone.

The strained relationship with my children was heart-breaking. The once vibrant and loving connection we shared had been tarnished by the upheaval of our family unit. Their silence spoke volumes, echoing the depth of their internal struggles and confusion.

It pained me to witness their suffering, to see their perception that the disintegration of our family was solely my fault. I longed to explain my life story. I carried the burden of their disappointment and resentment, understanding the magnitude of the impact my actions had on their lives. The delicate bubble of security and protection that I had meticulously crafted for my children had burst, shattering the illusion of an idyllic existence in which we had cocooned ourselves.

I realized that in my quest to shield and protect my children, I had unintentionally deprived them of the valuable lessons that adversity and imperfection can teach. Life, with its inevitable trials and tribulations, had arrived at our doorstep, and my children found themselves ill-equipped to navigate its turbulent waters.

I had failed my children – my role as a mother had both protected and hindered them simultaneously. I had failed to equip my children with the necessary tools to navigate the harsh reality of life. The picture-perfect façade I had cultivated had disintegrated.

I also failed them spiritually. I failed to bring them up in the knowledge of God. I fell short in nurturing their spiritual growth and guiding them in matters of faith. I did not prioritize their involvement in religious activities or provide them with a strong foundation in the church.

This realization continues to weigh heavily on my heart, as I understand the significance of spiritual development in shaping individuals' character and values. I acknowledge that my failure to instill a sense of spiritual guidance may have impacted their overall well-being and understanding, which later led to the unprecedented estrangement.

And so, I acknowledge that my actions had unintended consequences, and I accept full responsibility for the pain I caused. While I firmly believed that the dissolution of my marriage was necessary, I recognize that the manner in which it was brought to an end was deeply flawed.

I have paid the price.

CHAPTER 18

Dismantling the Marriage

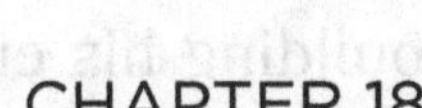

Surprisingly, my husband and I managed to have a civilized conversation about our impending divorce. We verbally agreed that I would be the one to leave the house due to the exorbitant expenses of maintaining such a large property, which I could not afford. He also promised to purchase a townhome for me and provide monthly alimony. The townhome was to be placed in my name as well as the children's names. Sadly, our agreement lacked written documentation, a reflection of my naivety and misguided trust in him — a significant error on my part.

Indeed, we had shared twenty-seven years of marriage and had jointly nurtured two exceptional children. I had been a dedicated mother to our children. The events that followed took me completely by surprise. I did not expect him to discard me so callously, as though I were merely a piece of old clothing. We had shared a lifetime and despite the storms, I had played a significant role in building his empire. Foolishly, I believed that we could maintain a friendly relationship, even throughout our separation and divorce.

And so, in the latter part of January and during February 2019, we began the search for a townhome or apartment in a gated complex. To my astonishment, my husband suggested that his friend's townhome, which I had previously visited, could be a suitable option for me. I was taken aback because the place was small, with low ceilings, a tiny kitchen and in a state of disrepair.

It was distressing to realize that my husband believed this subpar dwelling would suffice for me, especially considering our palatial home. The situation contradicted the law, which dictated that I should continue living in a manner to which I was accustomed. The signs were clear; the situation was becoming evident. The writing was on the wall.

I firmly expressed my lack of interest in his friend's townhome, leaving no room for ambiguity. Yet, my husband persisted in his unscrupulous tactics. He urged me to continue the search for a new home, and whenever I found a property I liked, we would separately drive to see it, even though we were leaving from the same address, all part of his elaborate game. I distinctly remember a situation where he instructed the real estate agent to submit a cash offer for a property I had shown interest in. The offer was made, but he never signed the document, leaving everything in limbo.

Simultaneously, my husband insisted that I see a psychiatrist of his choosing, Dr. Levy. Before my first session, my husband had a private meeting with Dr. Levy. During my initial session, much to my surprise, Dr. Levy diagnosed me with bipolar disorder – a diagnosis no other doctor had ever suggested.

I disagreed with this assessment, as it did not align with my own understanding of my mental health. Furthermore, Dr. Levy prescribed medications that could have side effects which impacted the brain, medications I was unwilling to take. Disregarding my objections, my husband would forcefully administer these pills to me, intruding into my bedroom at night. I have since come to understand that his actions were, in fact, a criminal offense. Still, true to my nature, I refrained from pursuing legal action, not only for this transgression but also for other unlawful behaviors he exhibited.

Instead, I became compliant and started to take the medications voluntarily except for one particular drug which I found had serious negative side effects on my sleep including hallucinations.

Living in the matrimonial home became an unbearable ordeal, filled with torment. My husband, no longer wearing the mask of deception, began pushing me out of the home, making it clear that I was unwelcome. Further adding to this troubling situation, my husband took it upon himself to forcefully snatch away my house keys, depriving me of the freedom to come and go from my own home. Feeling trapped and desperate for guidance, I sought the help of a divorce lawyer.

Reflecting upon why I tolerated this denial of my basic rights, I find myself at a loss for answers. At this stage, I could have involved the police, but in my effort to shield my children from public embarrassment, I chose not to involve them. I deeply regret that decision now. Since then, I have grown and evolved, and I will never allow my voice to be silenced again.

Instead, what I did at the time, was that I succumbed to the relentless emotional abuse, feeling powerless and defeated. No words can adequately express the excruciating pain that consumed my heart during those dark days. I was trapped in a cycle of pain and fear.

Caught in a situation I never could have imagined, I felt utterly lost. I was a bird caught in a gilded cage. Desperation consumed me, and a deep unhappiness settled within. Within the turmoil, Mark emerged as a wellspring of strength, offering me strong emotional support. With his sharp intellect and fearlessness, he stood in stark contrast to my own timid nature. He struggled to comprehend the inhumane treatment I suffered, especially considering I was the loving mother of my husband's children.

I needed to chart a new course. I stood at a crossroads, knowing I could not endure another month trapped within those suffocating walls. It was clear to me that relying on my husband to provide a new home was merely fiction.

The bitter truth settled in: my husband had no intention of treating me with fairness or kindness. I had become an unwelcome presence, subjected to his calculated vengeance. He had once again taken on the role of judge and jury, casting his condemning verdict upon me. It became apparent that I would be made to pay a high price for my perceived wrongs, trapped in a cycle of unjust suffering.

Taking charge of my life, I began the quest to find a new apartment to rent, marking a significant step towards independence. It was the first time I searched for a place without my husband by my side.

In the meantime, I confided in my three brothers about my distressing predicament. They offered staunch support and comfort which meant the world to me during such a trying time. I also summoned the courage to share part of my story with my mom, although I could not bring myself to reveal all the painful details due to the overwhelming embarrassment and shame I carried.

Each day seemed like a blur as I navigated through a mental haze, partly due to the medications I was taking and my mind's attempt to shield me from the harsh realities I faced.

During this transformative period, a connection formed with Mark. Our correspondence grew, and friendship and love blossomed. He became a source of affection, validation and understanding, providing an empathetic ear during moments of vulnerability.

At the time, Mark was refurbishing a home that he had recently purchased. He sought my advice and assistance in managing the project. It was a welcome distraction for me.

My husband continued to inflict misery upon me while I was still residing in the marital home. One particular incident stands out, where he deliberately restricted my access to the two printers that I regularly used. These printers were vital to my tutoring business, as I used them to print tests, worksheets, and study materials for my students. This action was a deliberate attempt to undermine my business, which was still in its early stages of development, and my sole source of income.

That was not the end of it, my husband went to even greater lengths to sabotage my business; disabling the air conditioning units in both my office, where I conducted my tutoring sessions, and my bedroom. I am still perplexed as to how he accomplished this, but the fact remains that I was unable to utilize these essential AC units. In my office, which lacked windows that could be opened, the AC was crucial for maintaining a comfortable environment for my students.

Disconnecting the AC units in my bedroom was an entirely new level of cruelty since, for the past twenty years, every family member had always slept with the use of the air conditioning. My husband was fully aware of my chronic sleep difficulties, and he knew that removing my access to air conditioning would make my situation worse. It was clear that he took pleasure in exacerbating my problems and causing me misery.

Overall, my husband's actions were not only aimed at causing distress in my personal life but he also deliberately targeted my budding tutoring business. He was also intentionally driving a wedge between my children and I. He removed all photographs hanging on walls which featured me either alone or with my children. It was as though he was trying to erase my very existence.

The monster in him was rearing its ugly head, once again. He was determined to inflict pain, embarrassment, and public humiliation upon me. Numerous derogatory statements were made by him, and I will recite a few of them for reference:

"You will be on the streets within one year of leaving me".

"Men will take all your money away from you".

"You will be married within one year of the official divorce"

"You are nothing but a slut."

These are just a handful of the disparaging comments he made, although some of them contradicted each other. His emotional imbalance was evident to me.

On another occasion I came home to find no-one at home, an unusual occurrence. I found myself locked out, left to wait for someone to arrive and grant me access to my own home. For nearly an hour, I waited outside my home until my husband finally arrived, granting me access.

While I will not delve into all the incidents that unfolded after news of my connection with Mark became known, it became dishearteningly clear that my children had become entangled into the complexities of the impending separation and divorce. This realization weighed heavily on me. I had earnestly wished they would not feel compelled or swayed to take sides, recognizing that the parent-child bond stands distinct from a marital union. Even though a marriage might come to an end, my role as their mother could never be torn asunder. Regrettably, I was proven wrong, and the signs of their alignment grew more pronounced with time.

Experiencing this situation has been the most agonizing trauma I have ever faced. Witnessing the strain on my relationship with my children has been deeply distressing, and it has challenged me in ways I could never have anticipated. My love for them remains steadfast, and I continue to hope for healing and restoration in our relationship despite the heartache we have endured.

On the day I actually moved out, in March 2019, my husband spitefully declared, "You will never set foot in this house again." To my husband's credit, he allowed me to take some of the furniture with me. I did not want to take too much, as I wanted my children to continue enjoying the beauty of the home and the way I had decorated it. So, I only took my bedroom furniture and a few other items.

When the movers arrived to assist me, my husband took it upon himself to involve our son in the process, asking him to photograph the items I was taking. This added yet another layer of disrespect towards me. It broke my heart to witness how my husband purposefully involved our children in the animosity surrounding our impending divorce. It felt almost criminal that he would manipulate them to treat me, their own mother, as if I were subhuman.

Even though my children were adults, they still depended on him to maintain their lavish lifestyles, which likely played a part in their disloyalty towards me. While I do not intend to excuse their behavior, I believe their naivety and the emotional turmoil and discord they were experiencing contributed to their actions. It was a painful realization.

Nonetheless, I still wished for them to have a positive relationship with their father. Even as I pen this book, that remains my heartfelt wish. I also wished that in spite of a divorce, there could have been an amicable atmosphere of mutual respect between my ex-husband and myself. Disappointingly, this aspiration has yet to manifest itself.

My husband's sinister and cruel intentions were apparent.

CHAPTER 19

Descent into Darkness

$\mathcal{T}$he journey following my departure from the matrimonial home proved to be an incredibly challenging and emotive experience. It wasn't merely the act of leaving behind a place filled with all the comforts and luxuries of life that posed the greatest difficulty; rather, it was the strained relationship I had with my children. Even with the presence of Mark and my brothers, I felt a sense of isolation that I had never experienced before.

While I was able to maintain communication through text messages, my children unyieldingly refused to visit me, or meet with me even though I resided just a five-minute drive away.

The overwhelming sense of loneliness I experienced was entirely new and utterly unbearable. Living alone was an unfamiliar territory for me, having never done so before. I had managed to find a small two-bedroom apartment to rent, with one of the rooms serving as my makeshift classroom. While the apartment was decent by general standards, it paled in comparison to what I was accustomed to. It signified a significant step down in terms of my living arrangements.

During this time, Mark remained an integral part of my life. He evolved into a lifeline that I relied upon for emotional support, understanding and companionship. With each passing day, our bond deepened, creating an unbreakable connection. He became an anchor in the turbulent sea of uncertainty.

We had established a routine where he would call me first thing in the morning and he would continue to check on me throughout the day. Mark's dedication to work often rendered him a workaholic, leaving little time for us to spend together.

Nevertheless, even with limited time, I never doubted that I remained his priority, and that sense of security was a different experience for me and was truly reassuring. We cherished each other's company and spent the weekends with each other.

As I adjusted to my new normal, in early April 2019, I was startled to receive a text message from my husband stating that he could no longer fulfill his commitment to provide me with a monthly allowance as previously agreed. He alleged being unwell and incapable of working. Initially, I felt a genuine concern, but soon I saw through his deceitful tactics. It was all a lie. It became unmistakable that I needed to take swift legal action to secure temporary financial support until the final divorce settlement could be reached.

I am a proud Jamaican; however, our legal system is woefully under-resourced, presenting significant challenges. Seeking legal resolution in this country can be an arduously protracted process, and I had hoped that my husband and I could have resolved matters without resorting to the court system.

Unfortunately, such hopes were obliterated as my husband had now reneged on his earlier promises. Being the one who left, I found myself at a disadvantage while my husband seemed to have everything working in his favor. Afterall, his lifestyle remained unaffected. It was sad to see how my misery became a source of amusement for him, as he reveled in my pain and struggles. Afterall, he had told me I would be on the streets in one year.

I started to feel a sense of panic as the urgency of the situation became apparent. Determined to take action, I promptly visited my lawyer's office seeking their expertise. Recognizing the need for immediate intervention, my lawyer initiated the process of securing a court date for an emergency hearing to obtain interim maintenance.

A date was scheduled for the end of May, providing a crucial opportunity to present our case. However, prior to the hearing, it was necessary to serve my husband with the original court papers, ensuring he was informed of the impending court date. To achieve this, a bailiff was engaged to carry out the mission.

The bailiff's diligent efforts failed to accomplish the task, as my husband proved elusive. He consistently refused to answer the doorbell situated at the gate, frustrating the attempts to serve him the papers. Realizing the significance of timely delivery within a fixed timeframe, my lawyers and I grew increasingly concerned.

In an attempt to overcome this hurdle, the bailiff decided to lay in wait for my husband, hoping for an opportune moment when he would leave the property. This strategy also proved unsuccessful.

With time running out, both my lawyers and I found ourselves wrestling with the pressing question: How do we ensure that the court papers are successfully served to my husband? An idea sparked in my mind, reminding me that I still possessed the gate remote. It occurred to me that my husband, being an early riser, would likely be in his home office by 5:00 am.

Sensing an opportunity, I discussed this revelation with my lawyers, and together we devised a plan: I would utilize my gate remote to enter the property, followed by the bailiff and a police officer riding in a car behind me, to ensure a safe and secure environment should any unforeseen incidents arise. Afterall, I was still part owner of the property.

With the plan in place, we made the necessary arrangements to put it into action. While I had concerns about how this course of action would impact my children, who would also be present at the house, I felt compelled to proceed, believing it to be the only viable option. And so, we executed our plan.

By leveraging the gate remote and implementing this strategy, we aimed to fulfill the essential requirement of serving the court papers on my husband within the prescribed time frame. It was a decision made after careful consideration, driven by the urgency of the situation and the necessity to progress the legal proceedings.

As we entered the premises, a sense of tension filled the air. When I drove in, I noticed my husband speedily closing the front door and hurriedly shutting his previously open office windows. With a purposeful determination, the bailiff approached the closed front door and explained the purpose of our unexpected presence. Minutes passed, until finally, my husband begrudgingly accepted the court documents from the bailiff through the back door.

Little did I anticipate the far-reaching consequences of this incident, as the aftermath unfolded in ways I could never have imagined. Immediately following the encounter, I discovered that I had been blocked from contacting my children through phone calls and that my son had blocked me from WhatsApp messages. My daughter had not blocked me from WhatsApp; but had now stopped responding to my messages. The abruptness and severity of this action left me devastated. It was unfathomable to comprehend that they would resort to such measures.

While the exact motivations behind their swift and devastating reaction remain unclear, I strongly believe that they perceived my involvement of the courts as an act of betrayal and that, since I was the one who chose to leave our wealth, I should bear the consequences. The depth of sadness and disappointment

I felt in response to this turn of events is immeasurable.

The day that followed held immense significance as it marked my daughter's birthday, a joyous occasion that should have been filled with love and celebration. My desperate attempts to reach out to her were met with heartbreaking failure. My phone calls were blocked and my messages were unanswered. The realization that I was unable to connect with her on this special day struck me with intense grief. It felt as though I had been abruptly cast aside from her life, an agonizing blow to my spirit.

In the depths of my despair, a sense of hopelessness and tragedy engulfed me. Overwhelmed by an unbearable sense of loss, I found myself uncontrollably weeping, unable to find comfort. The pain of being separated from my children in such a manner pushed me to the precipice of despondency, questioning the very purpose of my existence.

Living in a world without my children, their presence and love, seemed unimaginable and unbearable. Their absence created an emptiness that pierced my heart, leaving me yearning for their warmth and the irreplaceable connection we once shared. I found myself reduced to a mere semblance of my former self, a hollow vessel in the wake of their estrangement.

I began to desperately search for a way to bridge the widening gap and rebuild the fractured bond with my beloved children. I soon discovered that the obstacles I faced went beyond the tragic blocked communication my children had placed between us. In an unforeseen turn of events, not only were my children estranged from me, but they also severed ties with my mother, my three brothers, and anyone else with whom I had associated. The extent of their disconnection encompassed everyone in my circle, amplifying the isolation and sense of loss that I felt.

With desperation gripping my heart, I turned to my daughter's godfather, a man known for his fairness and integrity. In spite of his association with my husband as a client, he remained impartial and unbiased – an admirable quality that deeply resonated with me. I sought his assistance, hoping he could serve as a mediator to reach a financial settlement with my husband and that he could facilitate the reconnection with my children.

Undoubtedly, my daughter's godfather exerted his utmost efforts in navigating these delicate matters. Despite his determination and sincere intentions, he too encountered obstacles and neither a viable financial agreement nor a pathway to reuniting with my children could be established.

This experience further underscored the complex nature of the situation, as the deep-seated divisions and severed connections seemed resistant to any resolution. Notwithstanding the fervent endeavors of a fair and honorable intermediary, the circumstances continued to present insurmountable challenges, leaving me in a state of overpowering heartache and longing for the restoration of the bonds that had been severed. I was desperate as my worst fears had come to pass. I had been rejected and abandoned by the two persons that meant the most to me.

In my search for any potential avenue to bridge the widening divide, I even sought the support of the sole family member on my husband's side who remained willing to engage with me – his youngest brother's wife. Although she expressed empathy towards the situation, I soon realized that her words of understanding were not followed by any genuine efforts to actively assist in resolving the turmoil.

I was saddened to witness the lack of tangible action or intervention on her part, despite her apparent comprehension of the pain I was enduring. One would expect that, given the gravity of the situation, she and her husband would recognize the impact that my children's estrangement was having not only on me but also on their own well-being. I was disappointed as I felt that they did not genuinely care about their niece and nephew.

The repercussions of this estrangement reached far beyond my own personal anguish. It was evident that my children's decision to distance themselves from me carried significant emotional weight that would undoubtedly affect them as well. The absence of a united effort to address and alleviate this sad situation only added to the immense disappointment and sorrow I felt.

In moments like these, one hopes for the strength and wisdom of familial bonds to prevail, enabling compassionate actions that prioritize the well-being of all involved. Disappointingly, the realization that such support was lacking deepened my sense of isolation and underscored the painful reality of my fractured relationships.

And so, my descent into darkness began once again.

CHAPTER 20

The Monster is Unmasked

With no alternative left, the divorce settlement led us to the courtroom. Accompanied by my brother Steve, I stepped into the solemn halls of the Supreme Court, an unfamiliar territory I had never anticipated entering before. Steve's presence provided invaluable support during this daunting experience, offering reassurance amidst the sea of uncertainties.

Within the court's confines, the lawyers representing both parties engaged in negotiations, leading to an agreement. Although I held reservations regarding the agreed-upon sum of money, I acquiesced based on the advice of my lawyer. Regardless of my personal concerns, he explained that contesting the sum would result in significant delays within the court system, potentially leaving me without the much-needed financial support for months on end.

While I harbored reservations, I chose to comply with the agreement in order to secure some immediate assistance for my well-being. Navigating the legal landscape demanded difficult decisions, weighed against the backdrop of extensive delays that permeated the court system.

It is noteworthy to mention that upon my husband's arrival in the court lobby, he deliberately chose not to acknowledge my presence or that of my brother. The absence of even a basic gesture of civility spoke volumes about his decision to embrace animosity.

In reflecting upon this unfortunate situation, it is apparent that the choice to prioritize hostility over common decency not only underscores the broken nature of our relationship but also reveals a deeper unwillingness to engage in respectful communication. Extending courtesy and basic civility towards one another could have potentially paved the way for a more amicable resolution and would serve as a positive example to our children.

During the course of my new situation, I reached out to former friends and acquaintances who had fallen by the wayside, due largely to my husband's disapproval, another distasteful trait of a narcissist. What I discovered through these interactions were unexpected and damning revelations. Four female friends of mine came forward, sharing their experiences of inappropriate advances made by my husband while I was still in the marriage. Some of these advances had occurred decades before our separation.

To say that I was shocked would be an understatement. My husband had always presented himself as pure, portraying an image of a devoted and faithful husband. In spite of the troubling incidents involving the helper and the alleged attempted rape charge by his employee, I had never fathomed that he would have the audacity to make advances on my own friends.

One particular woman, a married doctor whom my husband had introduced to me, had always sparked concerns within me regarding his unusual interest in befriending her.

He had mentioned meeting her through his work and suggested that I host a dinner for her, her husband, and their daughter. Looking back, I couldn't shake the feeling that something was off. My husband, who was not known for his sociability, seemed unusually invested in this connection. I harbored deep concerns about his intentions. My instincts had sensed something amiss, but sadly, I dismissed those feelings at the time. Again, this underscores the value of placing faith in one's God- given intuition.

To my surprise, as I reached out to her, she willingly stepped forward, exposing my husband for the deceitful and despicable individual he truly was. She recounted his inappropriate advances towards her with immense disgust. We bonded over our shared shock and despair regarding my children's estrangement, as she was very much aware of how close we were. She even made a valiant attempt to reach out to them, albeit unsuccessfully. Since then, we have formed a genuine friendship built on trust and shared experiences.

The revelations of these women unveiled a darker side of my husband, shattering the façade he had carefully constructed. It became painfully evident that his infidelity and betrayal had a long history, extending far beyond what I had initially realized. My eyes were open to the depths of his deception thus reinforcing my resolve to move forward and seek justice.

Discovering the depth of deceit and manipulation I had unknowingly endured left me questioning why these friends had chosen to remain silent. While I acknowledge that they may have felt it was not their place to interfere in the dynamics of a marital relationship, I respectfully disagree.

As I consider their perspectives, I recognize the complexity of such situations and the difficulty they may have faced in navigating the boundaries of involvement. It is a nuanced issue, and the choices they made were likely driven by their own personal beliefs and considerations.

Nonetheless, the disappointment lingers, stemming from the realization that I had been left in the dark, unaware of the extent of my husband's transgressions. It reinforces the importance of open communication and the sharing of pertinent information among friends, particularly when it concerns the well-being and integrity of a relationship.

These disclosures carried a deep significance, offering me a much-needed release from the burden of guilt that had consumed me. For far too long, I had shouldered an overwhelming sense of blame, holding myself solely responsible for the downfall of my marriage and the estrangement of my children.

I harbored guilt over my encounters with the doctor and the subsequent exit affair with Mark. However, with these newfound admissions, a transformative realization washed over me: I had not imagined it, but indeed the cracks within our marriage had existed long before those events occurred.

It became unmistakably clear that the deterioration of our relationship stemmed from deep-rooted issues that extended far beyond any singular incident. The truth unveiled a complex web of discontent and unmet needs from the early days of our union. The challenges we faced were not exclusively of my own making. The marriage could not have been salvaged by my efforts alone, for these cracks ran deep and were a result of a mutual disconnection.

With this newborn clarity, I freed myself from the heavy weight of self-blame. I recognized that seeking more, desiring growth, and longing for fulfillment were not unsound aspirations. The dissolution of our marriage was not merely a consequence of my ache for something beyond the confines of our relationship. Instead, it was an amalgamation of various factors and unresolved issues that had plagued our union from its inception.

This realization allowed me to find peace in the understanding that I had done my best within a faulty and broken relationship. It was a collective responsibility to nurture and sustain our connection, and the weight of its demise could not rest solely on my shoulders. With this new perspective, I embraced a renewed sense of self-compassion and the belief that I had made the right decision for my own growth and well-being.

Notwithstanding my cognitive awareness of the situation, my heart remained shattered, unable to fully comprehend the sense of abandonment inflicted upon me by my own children.

As I reflect upon the therapeutic journey I had embarked on after my first suicide attempt, it is a tragedy to acknowledge that the very schemas unearthed during my cognitive behavior therapy – abandonment and rejection – mirrored the agonizing reality of my children's actions.

Their cold indifference pierced through my being, leaving an indescribable ache that words fail to capture. Joy became a distant memory eclipsed by the weight of their callous disregard. I found it difficult to imagine a future where my heart could once again find peace and experience the warmth of authentic happiness. Even now, my heart aches not only for my own pain but also for the hurt and pain that my children must also be experiencing.

Speculations regarding their decision to estrange themselves from me abound, leaving me with a sense of bewilderment and longing for answers. Some believe they have been manipulated or brainwashed, while others suggest that my husband's threat of withdrawing financial support coerced their compliance. There is also the real possibility that they collectively arrived at the conclusion that I am a flawed mother, thus choosing to exclude me from their lives. They may have been disheartened by my human mistakes, my departure from their idealized image of a perfect mother —a fact they could not bear to accept.

However, the truth may be something entirely different, and it remains elusive. I yearn for clarity and understanding, desperately wishing I knew the reasons behind their actions.

It is important to note that I did communicate with my husband, making him fully aware of the situation of their estrangement. I strongly believe that he held and still holds the power to alleviate the tension and foster a more amicable environment between myself and our children.

Instead of seeking resolution, my husband actively fanned the flames of discord. Throughout the ongoing court battle, my legal team received affidavits from my husband that contained reference to irrelevant emails exchanged between myself and Mark. While I am unsure of the methods used to gain access to my emails, I did wonder if my daughter twho had access to my email password, had shared this personal correspondence with her father or had given him my password. There were also additional details and that she may have also furnished him with.

Although these emails and materials held no relevance to the court proceedings, it was a poignant and heart-breaking reminder that my husband may have enlisted our own daughter as a participant in his crusade against me, and more importantly, that he wanted me to know this. A slap in the face!

It unveiled a lamentable aspect of his character, inflicting a deep sense of betrayal and sadness. It casts a troubling shadow on his true essence, raising doubts about his ethical behavior and the authenticity of his love for our children. A father who genuinely loves his children would not weaponize them against their own mother. Such actions are not only unconscionable but also deeply damaging to the innocent hearts caught in the middle of parental strife, leaving scars that could affect their emotional well-being and future relationships.

Acknowledging these sad realities is not easy, as it forces me to confront the magnitude of the situation and the lengths to which my husband was willing to go in his campaign against me. It further compounds the pain and reinforces the belief that the road to resolution and healing is fraught with obstacles and unexpected betrayals.

The monster is unmasked.

CHAPTER 21

Annihilation

On the occasion of my fiftieth birthday, I celebrated first with Steve and his fiancée at breakfast, followed by a concert attended with Mark. No phone call from my children reached me throughout the day, dampening my spirit. However, as the day drew to a close, a brief WhatsApp message from my daughter arrived, bearing the words "Happy Birthday."

While the gesture touched my heart, it was fleeting. An insatiable longing for a deeper connection persisted, as my reply went unanswered. In a state of desperation, I continued to intermittently reach out to both my children through text messages, earnestly pleading for a chance to reconcile and mend our relationship. These messages remained unanswered, a testament to their insolence.

The same echoed in my interactions with my soon-to-be ex-husband. Although he did not block me on WhatsApp, he chose silence, ignoring my messages. In my texts, I earnestly appealed for his involvement in bridging the gap between my children and me, along with urgent requests to expedite the conclusion of our financial settlement discussions – a plea for closure that resonated the emotional urgency within. I now realize how weak I must have seemed.

As the turmoil that consumed my life continued, I remained committed to my treatment under the guidance of Dr. Levy. During one session, he expressed a genuine desire to bridge the divide by reaching out to my children on my behalf. I vividly recall sitting in his office as he dialed my son's number. My son answered and Dr Levy said, "Good morning, I am Dr. Levy, your mom's doctor". Before he could continue speaking, the phone line went dead. My son had hung up the phone without even considering that the doctor could potentially have been trying to convey devastating news about my well-being.

The realization that my son had disconnected the phone call left me feeling deeply embarrassed, as I had never raised my children to be so disrespectful. I struggled to comprehend the change in their behaviour, unable to find an explanation for this transformation.

Undeterred, Dr. Levy proceeded to call my daughter next. Although she didn't abruptly end the conversation, she merely stated that she was busy and promised to return the call – a promise that ultimately remained unfulfilled.

These experiences served as poignant reminders of the painful disconnect that had taken hold within my family. The disappointment and sense of abandonment I felt grew more profound with each unheeded plea for understanding and reconciliation. It was my fervent desire to restore the fractured bonds, yet the walls of silence and distance persisted, leaving me demanding answers and longing for a path towards healing.

Throughout these trying times, I continued to find support from my siblings, my mother, and my circle of friends. Among them, Denise, who also happened to be my daughter's godmother, played a remarkable role in my life. Even though she lived some distance away, she made it her duty to call me both in the mornings and evenings, serving as a pillar of strength during a period marked by confusion and disbelief. Like me, she struggled to comprehend the circumstances that had unfolded. Janice, also made valiant efforts to reconcile my broken relationship with my children, though unfortunately, those attempts proved unsuccessful.

As Christmas drew near — the first Christmas I would spend without my children — a sense of panic began to settle within me. The holiday season, which traditionally symbolized togetherness and joy, now loomed as a stark reminder of their absence. It was during this time that Mark's absence was also imminent, as he had to be out of the country for approximately three weeks. Sensing my unease, Denise proposed the idea of a cruise around the Eastern Caribbean.

We would board the cruise ship in Puerto Rico, requiring us to fly first to Fort Lauderdale and spend a night there before continuing our trip. Understanding the financial constraints I faced, Mark volunteered to fund the excursion, with the hope that my deep longing for my children would lessen and that I could experience some joy at Christmas.

The prospect of the cruise provided a glimmer of hope and an opportunity to temporarily escape the weight of my situation. That was my fervent wish, yet, it was not to be so.

My mental state began to spiral downwards. Despite embarking on our early morning flight from Kingston to Fort Lauderdale with Denise, my heart remained heavy and devoid of joy. The physical separation from Mark compounded the immense pain I was experiencing, amplifying the grief that enveloped my entire being. The mere thought of navigating Christmas without my children proved to be an overwhelming and disorienting challenge.

As the day progressed in Fort Lauderdale, I felt an alarming sense of losing control, spiraling further into hopelessness. I wept uncontrollably, and an overwhelming desire to return home consumed me. The allure of the cruise we had planned faded into insignificance as I yearned for the familiarity and comfort of home. A deep sense of anguish enveloped me, and a barrage of intrusive and distressing thoughts, including thoughts of suicide flooded my mind pushing me to the edge.

In that moment, the weight of my emotional pain became unbearable, overshadowing any semblance of joy or excitement that the trip might have held. I was grappling with agony, struggling to find a glimmer of light amidst the darkness. I found myself struggling with the inexplicable rapid deterioration of my mental well-being, as if descending into a dark abyss.

Denise, recognizing the alarming state of my mental well-being, grew rightfully concerned about my ability to continue with the planned trip. She feared the potential risks of me being hospitalized in an unfamiliar foreign country and decided to address the situation. She reached out to both Mark and Steve, sharing her worries and seeking their input. After careful consideration, it was unanimously agreed that for my well-being, I should return home the following day while Denise continued the cruise alone.

Driven by her genuine concern, Denise took it upon herself to contact my son and inform him of my condition. She spoke to him with heartfelt sincerity, saying, "Your mom is currently in Fort Lauderdale with me, but she is unwell and will need to return home tomorrow."

It saddens me to share his reply, a response that pierced my heart: "I will have nothing to do with her unless she signs a court document discontinuing the legal action against my dad." It is important to note that Denise had not disclosed the specifics of my condition, nor did my son inquire about it. The gravity of my perceived transgression which had led my own children to treat me in this manner, remains a painful mystery.

Reflecting upon this heart-wrenching exchange, I am filled with sorrow and disbelief. The weight of my children's conditional love, contingent upon my compliance with their demands, is a heavy burden to bear. The deep anguish I experienced originated from the realization that my own children made the deliberate choice to distance themselves from me, seemingly devoid of empathy or compassion.

Their actions reflect a troubling dynamic where it appears they have taken sides, whether influenced by external factors or through their own cognitive decision-making processes. This realization raises countless questions about the reasons behind their detachment and the extent to which external influences have shaped their perceptions.

The following day, I made my somber return to my homeland, where Mark awaited me. He had originally planned to depart that morning but he rescheduled his flight for later in the day to ensure he was there to greet me. Additionally, my brothers made the trip into Kingston with my mother, so that I could be in their care after Mark left.

As Christmas day approached, a sense of sorrow weighed heavily upon my heart. The heartfelt endeavors of my friends and family to infuse the holiday season with joy proved futile in the face of my overwhelming grief. The sense of defeat consumed me, making it nearly impossible to envision a future where I could navigate life while experiencing such unrelenting pain.

Christmas day, meant to be filled with warmth and love, was overshadowed by emptiness. The magnitude of my anguish seemed insurmountable. Thoughts of suicide were rampant in my mind.

I was under suicide watch.

CHAPTER 22

The Year 2020

As the year 2020 arrived, my discontentment with my living conditions began to intensify. Recognizing my growing dissatisfaction, Mark kindly suggested that I explore the possibility of finding a new apartment that better suited my preferences and offered a more modern living environment. Following his advice, I began the search and eventually discovered a place that felt right. As fate would have it, my moving-in date coincided with the onset of the COVID-19 pandemic in my country.

Suddenly, our lives were thrust into the uncharted territory of an unprecedented global health crisis. The emergence of the COVID-19 pandemic added a new layer to my already fragile mental state, as the mandatory isolation and social distancing measures imposed upon us became stifling. The weight of seclusion, coupled with the uncertainty and fear that permeated the world, cast a shadow over my well-being.

These uncharted waters brought about immense challenges and upheaval. The pandemic mandated strict isolation measures, which further restricted my interactions and connections with others. It also meant that I saw Mark even less, as we, like countless others, were compelled to adapt to a new normal of remote work and the confinement of our homes.

The impact of the pandemic on my life was undeniable, reshaping my routines, and redefining interactions with the world. The physical and emotional isolation took its toll, amplifying the complexities of an already tumultuous time in my life.

In the virtual sphere, my tutoring business transformed into a solitary endeavor, intensifying the prevailing isolation. The lively group of students who once filled my makeshift classroom were now reduced to mere echoes and images on a screen. I longed for their warmth, affection, and the camaraderie we once enjoyed as I realized how essential those connections were to my sense of purpose and well-being.

Weekends offered a temporary respite from this seclusion as I would spend time at Mark's house. The companionship we shared brought comfort, and I took special delight in exploring his lush gardens, which offered a tranquil refuge from the overwhelming solitude.

Still, the descent into darkness continued, and the depths of my sorrow led me to seriously contemplate my own demise. I found myself continuously grappling with the weight of suicidal thoughts, which, paradoxically, began to intertwine with my sense of identity.

Death beckoned to me like a lifeline, a way to assert some semblance of control in a life that felt utterly out of control. I had lost control over the things that once gave my life meaning: I could not make my children talk to me, and I could not get the settlement I wanted from my soon-to-be ex-husband. The only power I felt I had left was the choice to end my own life. Suicide became a haunting escape plan in my mind, a way to finally find peace from the emotional turmoil I was in.

Distressed by these thoughts, I confided in Dr. Levy, who recommended hospitalization as a necessary step for my well-being. I struggled to accept this course of action and ultimately decided against checking myself into the hospital.

On July 4, 2020, while staying at Mark's house, I composed my final farewell letters. They were addressed to my children, my brothers, my husband, and Mark. In possession of a cocktail of prescription pills, I had already planned to take a fatal overdose on Sunday, July 5, 2020. The next morning, I woke up, went through my usual motions, including sharing a morning greeting and hug with Mark and savoring my cup of coffee. I retreated to the guest room where I slept, separate from Mark due to our differing sleep habits.

Inside the confines of that room, I meticulously counted the pills, weighing my choices with great deliberation. The delicate balance of taking neither too few nor too many tablets consumed my thoughts. Fearful of the possibility of vomiting the medication, I summoned all my strength to swallow what I believed to be the optimal combination and quantity. With each pill, I reassured myself that this was the only viable course of action, the sole means of escaping the ceaseless nightmare that had consumed my existence.

With resolute determination and bravery, I ingested the fatal dose I had chosen for myself. I made my way into Mark's room, where we hugged, Mark being unaware that in my mind this was to be our last physical connection. After bidding him farewell, I returned to my bedroom, climbing into bed. It was around 8:30 am, and from that point on, my memory ceased to exist. The events that transpired afterwards have been recounted to me, as I have no recollection of the remainder of that fateful day.

Mark, who typically indulged in a leisurely Sunday morning of relaxation and reading, did not notice my absence until around 1:00 pm. Concerned, he opened the door to my room and discovered me lying on the floor. How I had ended up there remains a mystery, as I was completely unconscious and nonresponsive. I can only imagine the panic that must have gripped Mark's heart.

Without delay, he contacted Steve, who at the time, happened to be located at a considerable distance from the city, requiring a lengthy one-and-a-half-hour drive. Steve insisted that Mark rush me to the hospital immediately, recognizing the urgency of the situation. It is worth noting that in the country where I reside, arranging an ambulance service would have taken considerable time. Steve also reached out to my other brother, Robert, who was similarly out of town. Steve then enlisted the assistance of Denise, who is a medical doctor. She resided four hours away. My brother John was out of the country.

In a remarkable display of collective effort and support, everyone worked together to ensure my survival. Above all, the divine presence of the almighty God remained steadfast, orchestrating the events that ultimately saved my life. It became abundantly clear that it was not my time to depart this world.

Both brothers quickly travelled into Kingston, while Mark swiftly took charge, rushing me to a private hospital. I can only imagine the immense physical and emotional strain he endured, carrying me down the stairs and gently placing me into his car.

Upon arrival at the private hospital, Mark was met with an unexpected reality – the facility lacked the necessary resources to handle a suicide attempt of this nature. They refused my admission but directed Mark to take me to the primary hospital in the country. Recognizing the urgency of the situation, Mark insisted that I be transported by ambulance. Thus, I was swiftly transferred from the private hospital to the primary hospital, with Mark following closely behind. The uncertainty of whether I would live or perish remained hanging in the balance, casting a shadow of doubt over my existence.

I lived.

CHAPTER 23

My Life is Spared

*D*uring this critical time, Denise made a brave effort to reach out to my son. Surprisingly, he answered her call and listened as she relayed the events that had occurred. Although his response remained minimal, he assured Denise that he would return her call. It seems that he shared the conversation with his father. Demonstrating commendable responsibility, my husband promptly contacted Denise, seeking further details about the situation. To his credit, I believe he urged both of our children to immediately make their way to the hospital.

Upon the arrival of my children at the hospital, they found both of my brothers already present, seated in the waiting area. Meanwhile, Mark remained by my side, answering questions from the attending doctors as they worked diligently to address my condition. Officially in a coma, I lay there, completely unresponsive to the world around me.

I was informed that my children walked past my brothers as if they were invisible, showing no level of acknowledgement or respect. They made their way directly to the room where I lay. In that moment, they assumed a sense of authority, as if they were the ones in charge of the situation. They were, after all, my next-of-kin.

The situation was indeed grave, as it was imperative for me to be admitted to the intensive care unit (ICU). However, the ICU was already at full capacity. Undeterred, both Denise and my daughter explored various avenues to secure my admission, even attempting to secure a spot in the COVID-19 ICU, which happened to be vacant at that time. The details of who ultimately succeeded in their efforts remain unclear to me, but I was eventually admitted to the COVID-19 ICU.

The following day, sometime in the afternoon, I regained consciousness. As I emerged from the depths of unconsciousness, I found myself surrounded by a team of doctors and nurses who attended to my well-being. They posed questions and although my recollection of the details remains fragmented, I do remember them inquiring about my name and the current year, as well as informing me of my location. I observed the presence of an intravenous (IV) line inserted into my neck, delivering medication directly to my heart, along with another IV in my hand supplying fluids.

I discovered that I was restrained, tied to the hospital bed, unable to move freely. My cellular phone was left behind at Mark's house, but I managed to recall his telephone number and requested the doctor to contact him. Steve was also promptly informed, and although he brought my phone to me, he was unable to visit me due to the prevailing COVID-19 regulations.

Additionally, I experienced an intense ache in my left thigh, prompting the medical team to investigate further. They discovered extensive bruising, indicating that when I had fallen off the bed at Mark's house, I may have landed on my left side causing the injury.

To my immense surprise, around 7:00 pm on the same day I regained consciousness, my phone rang with a long-forgotten ringtone. It was a call from my son. Overwhelmed with delight, I eagerly answered the call, happy to find both my children on the line. It was a moment that brought tears of joy to my eyes. I had not yet been made aware that they were informed of my situation or that they had made their way to the hospital the day before.

The very next day, they arrived at the hospital and were granted permission to visit me. Words fail to capture the depth of joy I experienced upon seeing them. Their presence exuded genuine concern and love, providing happiness in the midst of turmoil.

While my daughter had to attend school, my son returned later bringing me soup and coconut water. When I attempted to feed myself, my unsteady hands hindered my efforts. In a touching display of love and care, my son swiftly came to my aid, gently feeding me. It was a deeply moving gesture, affirming the depth of his affection. In spite of these moments of tenderness, the estrangement that persists between us even now remains an enigma that I struggle to comprehend.

My time in the ICU proved to be bearable, albeit challenging. The medical team provided me with essential physiotherapy sessions, while psychiatrists conducted interviews to assess my mental well-being.

Denise, understanding the gravity of the situation, made a dedicated four-hour trip to visit me, fueled by genuine concern. Regrettably, despite her medical background, she was initially denied access to see me. Regardless, thanks to the intervention of my children, they managed to persuade the authorities to grant Denise a brief five-minute visit. While still in the ICU, Janice was also able to visit for a brief five minutes with my children's intervention.

I must acknowledge with gratitude, that both my children rallied around me during this difficult time bringing me essentials that were necessary for my hospital stay. My daughter, then pursuing her studies in medical school, effectively communicated with the attending doctors about my condition. I was also informed that my son, maintained open lines of communication with both my therapist and psychiatrist, expressing his deep dismay that such a dreadful incident could have occurred under their care.

Moreover, my son took it upon himself to reach out to friends who were unaware of my situation, extending his efforts to ensure I had the support network I needed. Janice, shared that they communicated frequently with her, expressing genuine concern for my well-being, including fears of potential brain damage and kidney impairment which was a real possibility due to the substances I had ingested.

I was informed that my blood pressure had dropped to dangerously low levels, posing a significant risk of inadequate oxygen supply to my vital organ, the brain. The severity of this reality raised concerns about potential brain damage that could have occurred as a result.

Furthermore, because of the ingestion of a significant quantity of toxic substances, there was undue stress on my kidneys. Blood tests revealed alarmingly high levels of certain substances, necessitating careful and vigilant monitoring of my kidney function.

During my second night in the ICU, while I was conscious, my blood pressure experienced an abrupt drop, prompting a swift response from the medical team who administered a crucial adrenaline injection to stabilize my blood pressure.

A whirlwind of emotions engulfed me as I grappled with the realization that had it not been for divine intervention, my life would have met a tragic end. Still, even with the comforting presence of my children, a complex array of emotions clouded my thoughts regarding my survival. I wish I could say that I was overjoyed to be alive, I was not. I had mixed feelings about my survival.

Yet, during this turmoil, I could not ignore the unmistakable truth that, in spite of my meticulous planning, a higher power had intervened, charting a different course for my existence. It became evident that there was a greater purpose, a divine reason for me to continue on this journey of life. There was indeed purpose in my pain.

According to the hospital's protocol, once my condition had improved sufficiently, I was slated to be transferred to the female ward for a brief period before being discharged. Nonetheless, I had a strong desire to be transferred to the private wing of the hospital. To facilitate this move, a small deposit was required. As Mark and my brothers were occupied with their work commitments, I reached out to my son, who happened to be available at the time, requesting that he use his credit card to make the deposit payment.

I reassured him that I would promptly reimburse him. It's worth noting that my son's credit card was, in fact, provided by my husband. While I was aware of this detail, I could not have fathomed that my husband would disapprove such an arrangement. It was not an exorbitant sum of money.

In response, my son informed me that he would call me back shortly to confirm if he could proceed with the payment. I assumed he consulted with his father before responding, and when he did call back, he suggested that it might be more appropriate for one of my brothers to handle the deposit. I was taken aback by his response, as I firmly believed, and still do, that my husband had denied his request. This incident sheds light on the character of an individual to whom I was married for twenty-seven years, providing further confirmation of his malicious nature.

The fact that he would go to such lengths to deny a simple deposit payment, even when it was in the best interest of my health and well-being, further illuminated his spiteful intent and utter lack of empathy. It is a stark reminder of the toxic and oppressive environment I endured throughout our marriage, leaving lasting scars on my soul.

In spite of the gravity of my condition and the life-threatening situation I faced during my hospitalization, it was disheartening to realize that my husband, never extended a single call or text to me to inquire about my well-being.

While I did not anticipate his genuine concern or support, I was and will always be the mother of his two children. In fact, I was still married to him at the time. His complete absence during such a critical time underscored his lack of compassion and disregard for my suffering and showcased his true character for all to see. Even though we were separated, one would not have expected such callous behaviour.

Notwithstanding, I did appreciate his decision to send our children to the hospital. Although our relationship was strained, their presence provided a semblance of solace and a reminder of the love we once shared as a family.

Upon my discharge from the hospital, I carried with me a mix of emotions and a multitude of experiences, both good and bad, some of which I choose to keep private for now.

I was overjoyed to be going home.

CHAPTER 24

Life Continues

$\mathcal{U}$pon my arrival home, I faced the challenges of my physical recovery, particularly with walking due to the injury on my left thigh. Robert had kindly offered to take me home from the hospital, as my children declined to do so. The presence of my mother, who arrived the next day to support me during my recovery, provided some relief in the middle of the emotional turmoil. Though we did not delve deeply into our feelings, I can only imagine the heartbreak it caused her to witness the mental pain I was going through.

Returning to my apartment brought a whirlwind of emotions that besieged me. The lingering whispers of suicidal thoughts cast a persistent veil over my path to healing. Contrary to what one might assume, these thoughts didn't merely vanish. Even though the lines of communication had reopened with my children, the agony and torment I had been through, were not erased. They remained etched within my soul. I still struggled with making sense of what had become of my life. The drastic and sudden changes that had occurred were still reverberating through my being.

As an integral part of my recovery journey, I made the decision to welcome Daisy, a spirited five-month-old Shih Tzu puppy, into my life for emotional support. While I had never considered myself a 'dog' person, the influence of a neighbor introduced me to the idea of having a 'house dog'.

Daisy, as it turned out, was more of a handful than I had initially envisioned. However, she graciously filled my life with the unconditional love and companionship I longed for. Although she could never fully replace the human connection I needed, the bond we shared played a significant role in aiding my mental recovery. Pets offer immeasurable emotional support, providing a unique and irreplaceable source of comfort. Their companionship, boundless affection, and intuitive understanding have a remarkable way of soothing our hearts during difficult times.

Correspondence with my children continued through texts and phone calls, but they adamantly refused to visit me in person or to even meet me elsewhere. The reasons behind this decision remains elusive, leaving me to speculate and question. While their initial concern seemed genuine, it gradually waned as the weeks went by. Then, on October 31, 2020, both my children once again blocked me from their lives, with my daughter even choosing to block me on WhatsApp.

A tidal wave of disillusionment and distress crashed over me, their weight nearly unbearable. The absence of any explanation served to intensify my state of confusion. I can only speculate that their actions might have been provoked by the imminent court date on November 4, which marked the continuation of the legal proceedings for the ongoing divorce settlement. However, even that rationale appeared flawed upon closer examination.

Throughout our communication, neither of my children had broached the subject of my ongoing court with their father. As I recount these events, I struggle to make sense of it all, searching for answers that seem mysterious and leaving me with a sense of intense loss.

In the aftermath of my recent mental crisis and subsequent hospitalization merely three months prior, it felt incredibly harsh and deeply painful that my own children opted to distance themselves from me once again, and without explanation. It felt like a sharp stab piercing through my heart. Still, I cannot help but feel a sense of compassion and understanding towards them. I recognize that they, too, might have been going through their own turmoil and struggles that I may not have been aware of.

It is possible that they were contending with their own emotions, uncertainties, and pressures, which could have influenced their actions. While their decision to estrange themselves from me is deeply painful, I choose to hold onto the belief that their intentions were not rooted in malice but rather in the complexities of their own emotions and their own healing. It is with this compassion that I continue to hope for a future where understanding, forgiveness and reconciliation can take place. My love for them remains steadfast.

*****

As I write this book, I am acutely aware of the potential consequences it may bring. I understand that by sharing my story and experiences, there is a risk of causing irreparable damage to the already fragile threads of hope for reconciliation with my children. It weighs heavily on my heart to think that my words might further widen the divide between us, erasing any glimmer of a future where healing and understanding can take place.

Nevertheless, I feel compelled to tell my story, not only as a means of healing and finding my own voice, but also with the hope that it may shed light on the complexities of human relationships and evoke understanding and empathy in the hearts of others who may find themselves in similar circumstances.

It is my sincerest wish that, someday, my children may come to understand the depths of my anguish and the unconditional love that continues to reside within me. Regardless of the challenges we have faced, I will always welcome them with open arms.

As I recount my life, my foremost intention isn't to cause any harm or intensify existing wounds; rather, it is to provide a window into my personal voyage – complete with its trials, tribulations, and eventual growth. My aspiration is that this sharing might, in some way, someday, play a part in fostering a collective journey toward healing.

In our shared humanity, each individual carries a host of experiences, ranging from the tempestuous storms that threaten to consume us to the breathtakingly radiant skies that paint the canvas of our lives. We all navigate through the unimaginable trials that life presents, and through this navigation, we emerge not only intact but often imbued with a newfound resilience and strength that propels us forward.

With gratitude, I acknowledge that one of the most tremendous lessons I have learnt is the importance of placing the almighty God at the centre of our lives. For too long, I had placed my children at that centre, and while my love for them remains resolute, I now recognize the need to prioritize oneself through self-love, emotional well-being and spiritual fulfillment.

I now believe in my inherent right to embrace freedom and to thrive in a relationship that not only nurtures but also stimulates me, where my presence is valued and cherished. Love and care should be reciprocal, as I am equally deserving of the affection and care that I've generously given to others. For far too long, I endured deprivation of my essential rights – freedom to choose my friends, freedom to engage with my family, and freedom to achieve financial independence. This realization has been transformative, shifting my outlook and reinforcing my intrinsic value and worth.

I have come to realize that my identity should not have exclusively revolved around motherhood. I am a multifaceted individual with dreams, passions, and desires of my own. While being a mother will always hold a special place in my heart, I understand the importance of embracing and celebrating all aspects of who I am as an individual.

I had always held the belief that I had been a devoted mother to both my son and daughter. Yet, I've come to acknowledge that their viewpoint might diverge from my own. It is with a heavy heart that I come to terms with the fact that their perspective on my motherhood may not mirror my own. I am painfully aware of my imperfections and the grievous errors I've committed. There is a strong likelihood that my actions might have inflicted considerable embarrassment and suffering upon them, and in that, I deeply regret letting them down. I am genuinely sorry.

I am committed to remaining receptive to their viewpoints, as well as actively engaging in the process of understanding, healing, and eventually seeking reconciliation. I believe that through open dialogue, empathy, and a shared dedication to mending our relationship, we can forge a path forward that honors our bond as a family.

I am not perfect.

CHAPTER 25

Beyond Imagination

Christmas 2020 brought slight improvement in my mental state compared to the previous year. I hosted Christmas dinner and my brothers tried their very best to keep me occupied. It was bittersweet as I grappled with the absence of my children. As the new year 2021 emerged, my primary desire was to bring closure to the court proceedings. In June 2021, my soon-to-be ex-husband submitted affidavits in court in response to my maintenance support application, further adding to the complexities of the situation.

The document signed by him contained an astonishing array of falsehoods that surpassed all belief and imagination. My husband's affidavit presented a disturbing collection of perplexing and inconceivable scenarios that appeared to arise from a deranged mindset.

The assertions put forth were nothing short of astounding. My husband claimed that shortly after receiving spousal support, I relinquished my apartment to live with my partner, only to later resume renting again. His audacious claims extended to suggesting that our daughter underwent extensive medical treatment due to the trauma inflicted by the dissolution of the marriage. Furthermore, he insinuated potential involvement in witchcraft, obeah, or other occult practices.

The assertion, though, that truly left me in disbelief was his allusion that my children feared for their lives while I resided in our marital home. These baseless claims bear no resemblance to reality. The depths to which my husband's mindset has led him to concoct such unfathomable scenarios are truly bewildering. These fabrications not only distort the truth but also reveal the depths of his misguided state of mind.

It is a tragedy to witness his attempts to manipulate facts and construct a false narrative, showcasing a complete detachment from reality. These outlandish claims serve as a stark reminder of the challenges one faces when dealing with an individual so utterly disconnected from the truth.

The gravity of the situation is compounded by the fact that an affidavit is a public document, and these groundless claims could have long-lasting implications for our children. While I am well aware of my husband's extraordinary cunning ability to manipulate and twist the truth, I am left to ponder the state of mind from which these assertions arose. His affidavits give credence and support to my continued belief that I had been living with a monster for far too long.

To say that my unease escalated would be an understatement. The concerns I harbored for the welfare of my children intensified as I contemplated the nature of the individual they were residing with. The paramount issue was their safety, an aspect that still weighs heavily on my mind. Despite my apprehensions, I acknowledged that as adults, their choices were their own. I reassured myself that if they required assistance or felt endangered, they would find a means to reach out to me.

Throughout this challenging period of estrangement, I have had a handful of encounters with my daughter. In each instance, her greetings have been infused with genuine love and warmth. This paradoxical mix of affectionate meetings and the prolonged silence in communication has intensified my sense of confusion and perplexity. Now, in this chapter of my life, I continue to offer prayers for my children while simultaneously entrusting this trial to the guidance of the Almighty God. With staunch belief, I hold that I have poured my utmost effort into resolving this issue.

*****

Amid this emotional puzzle, my yearning for a semblance of independence persisted. Living in a rented apartment became increasingly dissatisfying, as I wished for the freedom to create a space that truly reflected my personal touch. In the latter part of 2021, recognizing the need for progress beyond the confines of the courtroom, I made the decision to change legal counsel, hoping to expedite a settlement process outside the confines of the courtroom. It had become painfully evident to me that navigating the court system could potentially extend for an exorbitant period of ten years or more.

As the end of 2021 approached and transitioned into early 2022, a settlement agreement was reached, albeit spread over an extended period. Although the settlement fell significantly short of what I could have potentially obtained based on my legal entitlements, I chose to accept it as a means of concluding the arduous process. My eagerness to close that chapter in my life and regain my freedom outweighed any monetary considerations. Money, after all, is not the sole measure of fulfillment. Let my husband cling to his wealth, and may it offer him the solace he seeks.

The conclusion of 2021 brought an unexpected and deeply distressing turn of events. In November of that year, my mother began experiencing health issues, and despite consulting capable doctors and undergoing the necessary blood tests, nothing unusual was initially detected.

It was not until Christmas Eve that we received the devastating news that she likely had acute myeloid leukemia, a form of cancer impacting the blood and bone marrow. Without delay, she was admitted to the hospital that very day. Christmas Day 2021 was spent visiting my mother in the hospital, a stark contrast to what I had anticipated. Due to COVID-19 restrictions, our visit had to be brief. Throughout this challenging time, we maintained communication with her doctor, who happened to be a family friend, as well as my brother John, who lived with his wife in another country.

The gravity of my mother's condition swiftly intensified as she developed pneumonia, necessitating her transfer to a hospital in Kingston. Throughout her hospital stay, she received transfusions in an effort to increase her platelet count. My brother John managed to arrive a few days later and was able to spend some precious moments with her. Unfortunately, due to the COVID-19 restrictions in place, we were unable to be by her side, which weighed heavily on our hearts. Tragically, on December 30, a mere six days after receiving the diagnosis, she passed away.

The sudden and unexpected loss of my mother during this trying time has left an indelible mark on our family. We find comfort in the memories we shared, but the void she left behind is immeasurable.

However, there is a part that I find incredibly difficult to comprehend and accept. Both of my children were informed about their grandmother's admission to the hospital and her subsequent passing. Even with this knowledge, neither my husband nor any of my children reached out during this painful time. It was their own grandmother we were mourning, and yet they remained distant and seemingly indifferent.

As the funeral arrangements were made, and everyone was informed, I held onto the hope that my children would show up to pay their respects. My hopes were shattered when they did not even make an appearance nor did they reach out to anyone in my family. It deeply saddened me to witness the presence of all the ex-wives of my three brothers, who showed their support during this difficult period, while I didn't even receive a single text message from my husband. The response, or rather lack thereof, from my children has left me feeling discouraged and disillusioned. I now question the very essence of who they are. I find myself wrestling with the realization that they could exhibit such cruelty and lack of basic compassion. I sincerely hope that their actions were not controlled.

The new year of 2022 ushered in a year of grief and conflict. I grieved the death of my mother and I continued grieving the loss of my children. I was also dealing with the wrapping up of my settlement and finalizing my divorce. In spite of all of this, I was able to purchase a home in 2022, which brought me much satisfaction. In November 2022, my divorce became final ushering a sense of relief and closure that I greatly needed. I felt absolutely no regret. I was and still am genuinely happy that I divorced that man.

Despite all this, my ex-husband tried to deliver a final blow to my spirit. Sometime after the divorce was finalized, I discovered that the legal papers authorizing the transfer of my interest in the matrimonial home to my ex-husband, were prepared by none other than my own son.

This sad revelation left me feeling deeply hurt and betrayed, especially considering my ex-husband had an entire team of lawyers at his disposal. It was distasteful and even bordered on being disrespectful in my humble opinion. It became agonizingly clear that this act was intended to deliver a profound insult to my dignity. Disappointingly, my son's compliance with this request only deepened the sense of betrayal, as it unmistakably showed where his allegiance lay.

Nonetheless, even with this hurt, I have come to accept my new situation, and even though the memories of my children are ever present, I have come to terms with my new reality. The love and care I have showered upon them shall forever remain an integral part of their being, forever intertwined within their very DNA.

Today, I am content, and I opt to perceive meaning within my hardships, acknowledging the enduring imprint that will remain once my journey on this earth concludes. I have lessened the influence of the estrangement's impact on my life, opting instead to forge ahead and embrace fulfillment through alternative avenues.

I wholeheartedly accept my roles as an educator, a mentor, a writer, and an author. I humbly acknowledge the privilege bestowed upon me to influence the lives of innumerable students for the better.

As I reflect on my life thus far, I can confidently affirm that my students have truly benefited from our interactions. They have sought not only academic guidance but also a nurturing presence, and I am grateful to have been there for them. While I may have experienced a temporary loss of my biological offspring, I take immense pride in the many other children I have had the honor to nurture and support. They have become my extended family, my surrogate children. Their growth and success bring me immense happiness and gratification.

My heart brims with joy whenever I receive messages of love from my former students on special occasions like Mother's Day, birthdays, and Christmas, even though they have moved on from my tutelage. These heartfelt expressions of affection remind me that the bonds we forged endure, and my influence continues to resonate in their lives. This connection fills me with a sense of fulfillment, reaffirming my enduring legacy.

In the realm of education, the role of a teacher extends far beyond the imparting of knowledge. It is a tremendous responsibility to shape young minds, instill confidence, and inspire a love for learning. It is a privilege that

I hold dear and cherish, knowing that I have made a positive difference in the lives of so many remarkable individuals.

I have unearthed my purpose through dedicating myself to my students. With the dawn of each new school year, a fresh chance emerges for me to shape lives and effect positive change. Guiding, motivating, and igniting inspiration among my students, I propel them to aspire for greatness. Alongside this, my ardor for writing has surfaced, and armed with this talent, I aim to craft a lasting legacy.

I will craft a lasting legacy.

CHAPTER 26

Forgiveness: No More Monsters

As I pen the concluding chapter of my narrative, I come to realize that my purpose is far from complete. Countless opportunities for personal growth and fulfillment await me on the horizon. Peering at the road ahead, I am filled with budding optimism, knowing that there may be bumps along the way, but I am stronger now, and I will navigate through them with resolute determination.

My aspiration is to bestow upon those whose lives I touch, a gift of love, strength and resilience. Through my writings, the pen becomes my voice, and the words woven into my books and articles shall endure as a testament to my passion.

In the chapters yet unwritten, I will strive

to embrace new experiences and expand the horizons of my own potential. Each day presents an opportunity to cultivate kindness, empathy, and wisdom, contributing to the betterment of the world around me. And as my story continues to unfold, I am committed to cherishing the connections I have formed, sowing seeds of inspiration and fostering a lasting impact on the lives I touch.

I humbly accept my God-given gift of teaching, not only in academic subjects but also in guiding others through the unforeseen challenges that life throws their way. I choose to share my story to inspire others, showing them that even the most mindboggling trials can be overcome. We have the power to conquer the monsters that haunt our lives and emerge victorious in the end.

Throughout this journey, I have come to appreciate the immeasurable value of having a caring and understanding network of loved ones by one's side. Without the affection and understanding of these loved ones, the burden of mental anguish can become unbearable, leading to a dangerous spiral of desolation.

Suicidal thoughts are not a rational solution or a means of escape. They are the result of immense emotional distress, coupled with a sense of hopelessness and a desperate desire for relief. The belief that suicide provides an escape from suffering is a misleading illusion that masks the underlying pain and prevents true healing from taking place.

During those dark moments of my life, I failed to see the potential for my growth and transformation. I could not envision a life without my children. I was trapped in a cycle of despair, convincing myself that suicide was the only way out.

With the passage of time and the support of my devoted network, I gradually began to realize that there were alternative paths to healing. It was through therapy, self-reflection, and the compassion of others that I discovered the strength to challenge those destructive thoughts and seek healthier coping mechanisms.

Suicidal thoughts are not a personal failing or a sign of weakness. Instead, they highlight the urgency and importance of seeking help and support. The presence of loved ones who listen without judgment, offer empathy, and provide a sense of belonging can make a world of difference. They can help reshape the narrative of despondency and foster a glimmer of hope in the darkest of times.

It is time that society as a whole, recognize the significance of offering support to those in need. We must prioritize mental health.

By promoting open conversations about this subject we reduce stigma, and by providing accessible resources, we can create a culture of compassion and understanding. Together, we can ensure that individuals wrestling with suicidal thoughts are met with the support they desperately need, fostering an environment where hope can flourish.

We all make mistakes. I have made far too many, but I believe strongly that these mistakes were necessary to mold me into the person God wants me to be. It is important that we forgive ourselves. We are but humans laced with imperfection.

Forgiving others comes naturally to me, yet extending that grace to myself has proven to be a challenge. I imagine nurturing my younger self, recognizing that extending forgiveness to that innocent child would be easy and effortless. Nonetheless, self-forgiveness remains a work in progress.

Accepting the forgiveness granted by the Divine, I carry on, aware that mistakes are an inevitable part of life's path. And so, I acknowledge that errors will continue to arise, and I must summon the bravery to forgive them as well. In doing so, I cultivate a deeper love for myself.

I extend forgiveness to my ex-husband, my children, and all those who have played roles in my life's lessons. The lens through which I view people has shifted; no longer do I see monsters, but rather individuals bearing their own wounds. They grapple with their inner struggles and personal demons. My wishes are sincere for their well-being, accompanied by prayers for blessings and salvation from a higher source. I am grateful for their presence in my narrative, for their integral place in my testimony that continues to unfold.

I am filled with a sense of gratitude for the lessons learned, the growth achieved, and the resilience that has carried me through. My story may not be one of fairytales and happy endings, but it is a story of personal triumph and the spirit to move forward through life's challenges.

In spite of the hurdles and heartaches, the love and support I received from my brothers, my friends and my extended family has provided a respite from the storms of my life. Their unswerving acceptance serve as a constant reminder that true family extends beyond bloodlines and that love transcends physical boundaries. The unconditional love and acceptance they offered were like stitches that mended my wounds.

There have been times of skepticism, where doubt abounded. I now have an unwavering faith in the divine orchestration of my life's journey. I have seen the interplay of events and circumstances that could only be attributed to a higher power. I continue to marvel at the intricate tapestry that is my life, woven by divine hands.

The struggle with suicidal ideation has lessened as I have grown stronger. However, it would be remiss to claim that these thoughts have completely vanished from my consciousness. They linger, like unwelcome shadows, reminding me of the depth of pain and vulnerability I once experienced. It is a complex battle, one that transcends logic and defies easy solutions. The truth is, the battle is deeply personal and it is continuous; where resilience is tested and progress is not always linear. While I remain committed to my growth and well-being, I recognize that the journey towards complete liberation from such thoughts may be a lifelong endeavor.

I have adopted the art of standing tall in the face of adversity, firmly believing in my inherent worthiness of respect and kindness. Gone are the days of allowing anyone to diminish my value, dictate my identity or strip me of my freedom. I now empower myself by setting and upholding healthy boundaries, fearlessly expressing my truth, and seeking the company of those who genuinely uplift and support me. I celebrate my strengths, acknowledge my flaws, and recognize that my worth is not determined by the opinions or actions of others.

That emptiness that once consumed me has given way to a new sense of purpose and inner peace. I am an example of resilience. My battles have been many, my losses have been plenty, but still I stand. I did not die. God is in my story. He has never left my side even in my darkest days. At last, I have found the purpose in the pain.

With determination, I look forward to the road ahead, fortified by the knowledge that through every storm, there is always the possibility of sunshine on the horizon and that the light of the Almighty will guide me through every step of the way.

My steadfast faith persists, whispering to my heart that one day, my children will find their way back to me. Within the depths of my being, a flicker of hope remains ablaze, fueled by the enduring love that binds us together. I firmly believe that time has the power to mend wounds and that forgiveness can pave the path to reconciliation. Even if they choose not to return, I am eternally grateful for the precious moments we shared, for they are radiant lights that illuminate this world. My love for them knows no bounds, transcending distance and time. It is a love that will forever reside within me, an everlasting testament to the depth of our connection.

The intricate web of synchronicities and miraculous alignments that has been my life story, are reminders that I am not alone on this journey.

I am a masterpiece painted by the divine artist.

One thing is sure... God is in my story.

THE END

About the Author

$\mathcal{I}$ntroducing Dr. Karla Hylton, a highly esteemed educator and author hailing from the vibrant Caribbean nation of Jamaica. With a deep passion for teaching and mentoring, Dr. Hylton has dedicated her life's work to nurturing young minds and shaping the future generation. Her commitment to education extends far beyond the realm of academics, as she wholeheartedly believes in fostering the holistic development of each and every child.

Armed with a PhD in Biotechnology, Dr. Hylton has seamlessly integrated her scientific expertise with her strong belief in the transformative power of education. She views education as a catalyst for change, capable of reshaping lives and opening doors to endless possibilities. In addition to her scholarly pursuits, Dr. Hylton has ventured into the realm of writing, penning captivating children's books and exploring various genres that have captivated readers of all ages.

Dr. Hylton's literary creations reflect her creativity and her commitment to instilling valuable life lessons through storytelling.

Other Books By The Author

FIND THEM ON
amazon